Need Change?

Customer Service Tips to Grow
From Good to Great!

Written by Jean Steel

Illustrations by Suz Roehl
Edited by Susan Stewart

This book is dedicated to **Ed Cox**, my mentor and friend. I regularly meet people who inspire me, motivate me and challenge me. Sometimes I am fortunate to meet someone who does that and more, who actually changes the course of my life. Ed Cox is one of those people.
Thank you Ed, from the bottom of my heart.

Cartoonists:

Dan Piraro "Bizarro"
Tim Peckham
Randy Glasbergen
Cathy Thorne "Everyday People"
Mark Anderson "Andertoons"
Bert Silva "Bottoms Up"

Copyright 2015 © JEAN STEEL
Published by PSan Publishing. Printed in China.
ISBN 978-0-9831238-5-9

Table of Contents

Gratitude

This book would not have been done without Susan Stewart. She is the genius writer and editor that I am so fortunate to work with, yet again.

Of course I want to thank my family. Especially Suzie who once again did the amazing artwork for this book. This time I paid her. I discovered saying, "YOU have been chosen to do the artwork for my book. How lucky are you?" does not, sadly, work more than once.

Patrice my publisher from PSAN has the most mind-blowing eye for color, artistry and layout and just as important she is so easy to work with *and* made this project fun. My graphic artist Jennifer Star IS a star. Jenny Molinar, my wonderful assistant/partner in crime (you don't know how true that last part *almost* was) and Barbara Howard, my proofreader, also have my profound gratitude and friendship for life.

I also want to add my thanks to my Treehouse family. Treehouse is a group of entrepreneurs who meet monthly to encourage and learn from each other, laugh (A LOT) and kick butts when needed. Authentic feedback with love. So Ed Cox, Adi Ringer, Charmaine Peterson, Ed Cuming, Hayley Townley, Laura Krueger, Tom Parker, Sue Prior, Sammy Papert, Robyn Letters and Patrice - thank you. You know I love you all to the moon and back.

And finally the good, the bad and the ugly of the customer service that I encounter every day makes this book what it is. Which makes me laugh, shake my head, say (OK yell) the f-word *and* do my happy dance—the variety is astounding.

Meeting Dr. T.

a perky nurse
wearing green scrubs
and a counterfeit smile
popped in after ten minutes
to let her know two things

the gown opens in the front
and
he was running about an hour late

so she sat
contemplating
the fate
of the two bare feet
she was dangling
over the side
of the exam table

she'd recently had
her first proper
pedicure

a gift
from a friend
who didn't know
what else to do

impatience
sat swinging
perfectly polished
bright pink toes
trying
to keep time
to the heinous
canned music
in the small
cancerous room

I guess
she must have
been staring
at the floor
when he finally
opened the door

smart brown loafers
with fragile tassels
walked confidently
across ugly speckled
linoleum tiles

he sat softly
in a sterile chair
beside her

beige paisley socks
peeked out
from the bottom
of neatly pressed
khaki trousers

she rocked forward
reached out
a sweaty hand
to meet his

all the while
trying to ignore
the stinging commotion
of surgical grade staples
scraping against
the stiffness
of a blue paper cape

that opened in the front
where the rest of her

used to be

Why "Need Change?"

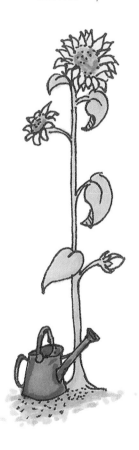

This is not a ho-hum book about a ho-hum subject. But when it comes to titles, *The Customer Service Manual* is about as lackluster as they get. So as with most things in my work, the title *Need Change? Customer Service Tips to Grow from Good to Great!* was born from personal experience. The fact that it carries a double meaning is icing. As a frequent restaurant customer, I am dismayed when my server presents the check, takes my money, and then asks, "Need Change?" That question is a bad habit that indicates either laziness or the presumption of a tip or both, and will end up producing the opposite result. Servers should never ask that question. Are laziness and bad habits producing negative results for your company? Could your company *need change* in the way you treat each other and the outside world? Clever, no?

Introduction

About a dozen years ago, I got a call from a hospital rep interested in hiring me to do a customer service training. I told him thanks for thinking of me, but customer service was one topic I didn't cover. A month later, I got the same request from the same guy . . . who got the same reply. Customer service? Nope, I don't offer that.

He was persistent (a quality I like). "We think you do," he said.

I thought about it. Every day, I'm a customer somewhere, and I do notice how I'm treated. But, being aware doesn't make me eminently qualified to teach it, does it? I teach communication. And attitude. And listening. And body language. And dealing with difficult people.

Wait, maybe I *do* teach customer service.

So, I met with the hospital CEO and agreed to develop and teach their customer service program. I read lots of books, learned the principles, and infused my existing workshops with current customer service stats, fun facts, and scary/funny true stories. In the end, what I wanted to impart—to them *and* to you—is the critical difference between good customer service and great customer service. You ready? If you love what you do, if you are positive, if you communicate well—that's good. If you go above and beyond, a practice usually fueled by an excellent working environment and supportive management—that's great.

So, how do we get to be great? My course consisted of gentle reminders to be present. Enthusiastic. Happy. Be aware of your nonverbal communication. It's truly amazing how loudly our bodies talk—and how oblivious we are of that fact! Don't use trigger words. "It's our policy" is not an explanation; it's a dismissal. Use your brain. Be nice. Yep, I did need to add that last direction. Here's why:

Remember the video/music stores? Before the advent of fire and the invention of the DVD, I used to be a regular customer at one. The clerk who checked out my videos was a young kid, and it was obvious he was bored breathless in what was likely his first job. He never looked me in the eye, he never spoke above a mumble, and he had perfected the *"life-sucks-and-I-don't-even-have-the-energy-to-give-a-damn"* sigh. On this particular visit, as he bagged my selections and handed them to me, he mumbled something I didn't catch.

"Excuse me?" I asked.

"I **said**," he announced, annoyed, "Have a nice day."

"Why did you say that?" I wanted to know.

"I have to," he admitted.

"I'm not feeling it. Do you really mean it?" I teased, smiling. Instead of the smile I had hoped to get in return, I got nothing but a confused stare. I left with a feeling not too far from despair.

Just saying the correct words is not customer service. **Meaning** it is!

So, exactly how do we cultivate the fine art of "meaning it," and how do we teach it to others? By learning to be happy. By deciding to be happy. By practicing that choice daily, sometimes hourly.

Here's a happy thought: The same principles and practices that help you offer exemplary customer service also help you become a better person. There's a saying: "Happy Work, Happy Life." (Actually, it might be "Happy Wife, Happy Life," but I like mine better.)

Years ago, I worked with Patty, a negative and exhausting woman. Patty's particular talent was her ability to go from whiny and complaining (her natural state) one minute, to chillingly cheerful the next. "So then my lazy husband had the gall to go out with his buddies . . . " she'd be telling us some mind-bendingly boring tale of household woe, and then the phone would ring. Patty would answer it with a sing-songy, "Helllooo! May I help you?"

What?

She was supernaturally nice (totally fake—I promise you) to the customers, but brutally annoying to her co-workers. Patty wasn't a team player.

Research shows there is a direct correlation between how staff members treat each other and how your external customers are treated. Most people aren't as talented as our Patty, who could turn her different selves on and off like a light switch. Ever get a chewing out from your boss and then have to make a customer happy in the very next breath? Hard to do.

So, I added something about teamwork. Call it "internal" customer service.

That video you watched at your employee orientation, or even that great motivational speaker your staff heard last year, does not guarantee the entire company is good to go on customer service. It's like learning a language. You can study Spanish with the best teachers money can buy—for years. You can become fluent. But, if you don't practice it, and *regularly*, you'll forget how to say "customer service" before you can say "adios corporacion."

Aristotle (yes, Aristotle!) said it best when he said: *"We are what we repeatedly do. Excellence then, is not a single act, but a habit."*

In the following chapters, you'll get brand new lessons about listening, logic, and body language. You'll read the newest numbers on stress, smiling, and a new kind of service—serving the "internal" customer. You'll explore the unlikely relationships between customer service and making assumptions, the passion factor, and empathy. There will even be short courses on telephone and email etiquette. You'll also read some startling stats about tales told and retold, the sometimes lethal damage caused by just one negative experience, and the astonishing power of online reviews and reputation management.

The world of commerce has gone global. So much so, that whether you own Dave's Plumbing in Littletown, Oklahoma, or the Plaza Hotel in New York, one bad customer experience story can be spread to thousands in minutes. In these daunting days of Facebook, YouTube, Twitter, and Instagram . . .

You really do need to care about customer service.

Chapter 1

WHY CUSTOMER SERVICE?

Why a training? There's a book? Really? I can hear the objections.

- "I've been here twenty-four years. I can't change now."
- "Some people are never satisfied."
- "People will still complain."
- "I am not going to be phony."
- "I'm too busy."
- "It's ridiculous, we *know* what to do."

Okay. I believe you. Let's take a test.

Correct thing to say, or not?

You probably got these two right. The thing is, a lot of customer service is obvious. I don't have to tell you not to use foul language, push people, or roll your eyes (well, I might be reminding you about that). You already know to avoid sarcasm, to make eye contact and to control the impulse to drum your fingers on the desk. Don't you? Yet even though everyone claims to know, poor customer service still is rampant. Rule number one, sometimes the best customer service is: Don't say the first thing that pops into your head.

Customer service is about being genuine. You can't fake genuine. If you are not a "people person" and you work with the public, shame on your hiring manager. And you are right, some people are never satisfied, no matter what you do. Even when you give them what they want. Some people just enjoy complaining. It's their natural state. But here's the reality (and I got this from a 5-star server who worked her way up from slinging hash at a diner during a 30-year career): *"The complainers are rare. Ninety-nine out of 100 of my customers are wonderful. I've never understood the servers who let one grumpy patron wreck their whole night."* So for the vast majority of people, being genuine works. Don't waste time agonizing over the small percentage you will never please.

There is a customer service tip called "the illusion of time spent." Let me give you an example. When a physician enters your room, stands in front of your examining table (while you grip the back of your paper hospital gown in a futile attempt at modesty) and flips through your chart, he might glance up at you occasionally, as he or she assesses your condition. You've gotten pretty good at guessestimating the time the doctor spent with you. Wasn't much, was it?

However, if the physician comes in, sits down level with you, looks directly at you, and listens to what YOU have to say, you are likely to guesstimate that he or she spent much longer with you, sometimes *twice* as long, EVEN THOUGH THE TIME SPENT WAS EXACTLY THE SAME in both scenarios. When we feel listened to, and the focus is on us, it feels good. And interestingly, it feels longer.

Customer service training isn't just about looking at what isn't working; it's about celebrating what is. And finally, it's remembering what Horst Schulz said: *"Unless you have 100% customer satisfaction, you must improve."*

Do YOU
see customer service
as the key to the success
of your business?

Do ALL STAFF
see customer service
as the key to the success
of your business?

Chapter 2

Who Me?

Yes, You Do Need to Care About

Customer Service

"The customer experience is the next
competitive battleground."
~ Jerry Gregoire

Here's the in-your-face case for putting customer service *first*:

- By 2020, customer experience will overtake price and product as the key brand differentiator.
- 89% of consumers have stopped doing business with a company after experiencing just one incident of poor customer service.
- One in four customers are dissatisfied.
- Only one out of 25 of those unhappy customers will ever tell you that they are dissatisfied, but they *will* tell others.
- 55% of customers would pay extra to guarantee better service (Did you know that's how the practice of tipping got started?)

- Attracting a new customer costs five times as much as keeping an existing one. So, keeping your current customers is the best way to do business.

Need more? Okay!

1. You Want to Stay in Business

Dramatic, yes. But true. People will not only pay more, but they'll also drive farther for good customer service. There are more than 250 general dentists in my area. We have a population of 275,000, so I have many to choose from. Why should I choose you? Whether you're a dental office, a tire store, a jewelry shop, or a gym, think about the reasons I should choose your business over all the others. Is it your convenience factor, your lower prices, your location, your ad campaign? Nope. Most research shows it's your *service*.

And, don't think that just because you're the only game in town you're safe. Especially if you are discretionary. Maybe you *are* the only pottery painting shop in town. But listen, if you're not nice to me, I don't really have to paint pottery. I can learn to blow glass instead.

I chose my dentist (Dr. Ryan Ross, DDS) because he is handsome. Duh! Actually, he is a great dentist. I honestly don't know whether he's a fabulous clinician or not, since I wouldn't know a good dental practitioner from a bad lion tamer. I didn't go to dental school. But, I do know how to recognize a man who is really nice, who really listens, is honest, trustworthy, on time, empathetic, funny, and lets you be a partner in the decision making process. Everyone in his office is cut from the same cloth, and that sealed the deal. Dr. Ross's business is booming because when people like you, they tell others, and that's worth more than the best advertising campaign money can buy.

So, how do I choose a place to do business with? I ask around. And, when I find one I like, I tell my friends, and I write Yelp and Facebook reviews. And, if I don't like them? Oh yeah, I do the same.

Business Insider compiles an annual list of the companies who scored the worst in customer service. Can you imagine the embarrassment? Yet, one of those companies has *never* done a customer service training for its staff, either before or after their name showed up on this list. As "the only game in town" they'll survive . . . but not for long.

2. Stress Reduction For All

Happy employees are more engaged, more passionate, and more creative. They take more initiative, and yes, they are more *productive*. There is a lower turnover rate, less absenteeism, and from there . . . you can become known as the company to work for. I work with Nikkei Concerns, a wonderful retirement community in Seattle. Their motto? "Making every day the best day." Another company I know has this one: "The answer is yes." The entire staff has been taught to cultivate a can-do attitude. When a customer has a question or request, employees want to say "yes" whenever possible. Even if it's a tall order, the internal response is, "This will be a tough one to pull off, but let's see if we can find a way." When every member of your company has making each day their best as their motto, and sincerely wanting to say "yes" as often as possible, poor customer service simply cannot survive. Hello, great customer service! Hello, success!

A famous television ad asks: "What's in your wallet?" I ask you: "What's in your motto?"

3. Good Risk Management

Friends don't sue friends. If they like you, they consider you a friend. In business, the way you handle problems and complaints is critical to cultivating and keeping your customers—your friends.

Years ago I was at a restaurant, took a bite of my salad, and chomped down on a huge staple. I called the waiter over, and he said it was from the box of lettuce; he immediately called the manager over. The manager introduced himself, apologized, and asked if I was all right. Yes, I was. Then, he said he would like to comp our meal. Nice. Problem resolved.

Another time, I was at a different restaurant eating lunch, picked up a french fry and saw a melted pushpin stuck to it. I called the waiter over and his reply was, "We have a bulletin board behind the fryer, and things are always falling off it." Wow! I asked for the manager, but he was too busy to come over. Now, if I were the suing type, this is who I would have sued.

4. Expectations Created from Other Businesses

Fair or not, most people will judge your service compared with other companies they've worked with. When I fly a certain airline, I am not just comparing them to other airlines, but to other companies I've done business with. If a phone rep treats me well at American Express* and I call and order a pair of shoes at an online company, I do compare the customer service. Apples and oranges you say? I think not. Customer service is customer service no matter where you are. Apples to apples!

I decided to use American Express in this example because I have never had a bad phone encounter with them. In fact, every representative has been stellar. Are you listening AmEx? Don't make me jinx myself!

In one survey, 63% percent of companies expected to spend significantly more on customer experience in 2014. Was yours one of them?

5. People Talk . . . People Write

People love to tell stories. The more dramatic the better. (Did you know that when we have a good customer service experience, we tell maybe four to seven people? If it's bad, that number jumps to from nine to 35! That's what the research says.) And because we like to tell a *great* story, well, the tale can become embellished over time. So what started, for example, as a smarmy smirk from a cashier can end up (twenty repeats later) that she smacked you in the face. A great story? Yes. True? No.

If you live in a big city, a bad Internet review or comment on any social media site can hurt you. If you live in a small town, it can shut you down. I tell people: "Behave as if you knew you were being watched." Because . . . you are.

6. That Enjoyable Boondoggle

It's only a few years old, but it has changed the world. Care about customer service because that thing we can't imagine living without, "the unimaginable imagined,"—the Internet—is here to stay.

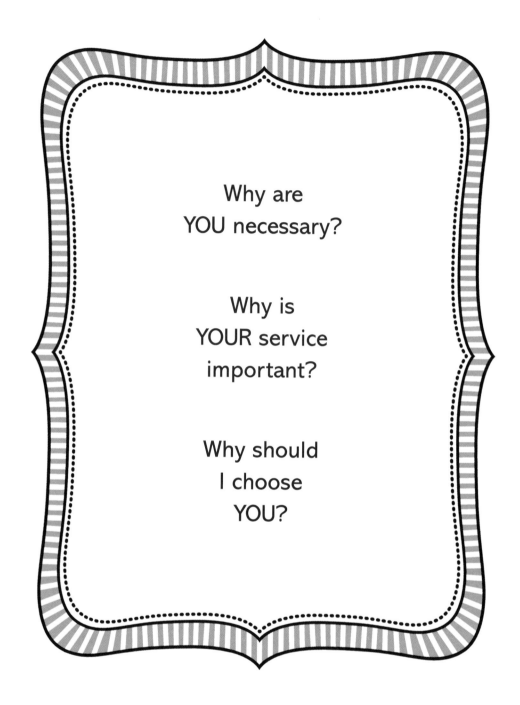

Why are
YOU necessary?

Why is
YOUR service
important?

Why should
I choose
YOU?

Chapter 3

"United Breaks Guitars"
Your Reputation on the Internet

Dave Carroll is a Canadian musician whose guitar was badly damaged during a United Airlines flight in 2008. Frustrated with the company's indifference over the incident, he asked himself: What would Michael Moore do? And then he wrote a song titled "United Breaks Guitars." Posted on YouTube, it amassed over 150,000 views in one day (it currently has more than 14 million), which prompted United to contact Carroll. It resulted in instant success for Carroll and a public relations nightmare for United. In 2011, *United Breaks Guitars: The Power of One Voice in the Age of Social Media* was published. If United had done the right thing initially, if it had apologized and paid for Dave Carroll's guitar, none of this would have happened. Which begs the question: What is *your* reputation worth?

The Internet is another reason why you need to care about customer service. *Time* Magazine wrote, *"Before the Internet connected the entire world, your business reputation was something you built, not managed. Fallout from the customer complaints you couldn't fix was of limited scope. Today, the Internet acts like a lens that magnifies every blemish, perceived insult and mistake—and then broadcasts it with a bullhorn."*

The internet gives angry customers a megaphone!

So, the Internet's effect on customer service is twofold: The first is the immediacy of allowing unhappy customers to post and have it read by thousands. The second is the choice it offers: I can order it online if I don't want to go into your brick-and-mortar store.

We can easily read about you on Yelp, Google, TripAdvisor, and Angie's List. Some unhappy customers have even started "I hate XYZ Company" Facebook pages. So many, in fact, that there are probably several you would happily join. Walmart? Chevy? Florida State Seminoles? Already there. There is even an "I hate Facebook" page on Facebook.

A friend of mine wrote a Facebook update about her college, describing her travails in getting a copy of her diploma. She named the college, a popular one with many of my friends. Not so much . . . anymore.

In 2014, an unhappy Comcast customer decided to record an 18-minute call with an employee when he tried to disconnect his service. When I Googled it, I got over 145,000 references. There it was . . . on *Huffington Post, Business Insider, Business Week*, ABC News, NPR, and many more.

In 2012, a Burger King employee was fired after posting photos of himself stepping into lettuce bins with his dirty shoes. Can you say "public relations nightmare"?

Today, corporations who have the bucks are spending half their marketing budgets to hire agencies that do nothing but manage their online (Internet) reputation. Never underestimate the power of the Internet.

Remember—Internet customers:

- Have other alternatives
- Are more selective
- Have access to more information
- Have more choices

Before I work with a company on customer service, I check them out online. (Well, wouldn't you?) Interestingly, many of the companies have never looked at their online reputation. Besides the obvious Yelp, there are web pages that deal solely with specific kinds of companies. When I was working with an online college, I looked them up on five different review sites.

Almost every time I stay at a hotel I review it on TripAdvisor. Why do I take the time? Because I use the site myself to help select a location, so I appreciate the feedback others give. I seldom receive a reply to my comment—and the vast majority of my reviews are positive! When someone says they like your shoes, don't you usually say "Thanks!"?

How about you? Are you saying "Thanks!"? Are you managing your online reputation? Do you have Google Alert set up so when someone writes about you, you can see it? Do you use a reputation management service?

Take your online reputation seriously. Take it from those who have lived and, I was going to say learned, but some of them died before they got the lesson. The Internet can, and does, make and break businesses every day.

Are YOU
managing your
online reputation?

Do you
have Google Alert set up
so when someone writes
about YOU,
you can see it?

Do YOU
use a reputation
management service?

Chapter 4

Customer Logic
& Chain of Experience

Customer Logic . . . It Isn't Logical!

Customer logic is an element of customer service that is badly misnamed. Because the principle of customer logic is anything but. Here's what I mean:

I was walking down the hall of a hospital where I worked and was stopped by a woman. "Excuse me, do you work here?" "Yes," I smiled. "Do you know what time the bus stops out front?" (Actually, I didn't even know we *had* a bus that stopped at our hospital.) I was a health educator, not an information desk. "I'm not sure," I said pleasantly, "but let me find out." Her reply? "I thought you said you worked here."

Customer logic assumes that as an employee you should know everything about every aspect of your business. Think about it: How many times have you been asked a question regarding some obscure fact about your company? I know a woman in apartment sales who was asked how many partners owned the corporation she worked for, and where did they live? And a response was clearly expected.

We can't be expected to know everything. I suggest you follow up all those impossible questions with "Let me find out for you." Then, find the person (every company has one) who knows everything about everything. There's a great TV series called *Suits*, with a character—a secretary named Donna—who has answers for questions no one has even asked. She's just a TV character, but I know there is a "Donna" in every office. And here's the plus—if you've seen the show, you know that Donna delivers her knowledge with confidence, never smugness. Another great customer service tip . . . But I digress.

Customer logic also decrees that "You, the employee, *are* your business." Think about that. You decide to take a college class, and the admissions gal is rude, condescending, and abrupt. You leave annoyed and hating the college. Not the person, but the *college*. You've just allowed one rude person to define the entire entity. Your knee-jerk emotional response to that experience is "I hate that place." Right? So what do you hate about it? Generally, it's just one thing, and that thing is often a person. What you have done is called "customer logic"—thinking the person is the business.

Customer logic can extend away from a person to include other company affiliates, like signs and vans. I once witnessed a plumbing van driving like a maniac on the freeway. ACME Plumbing (not the real name) was written in large, bold letters that covered one whole side of the van. "I won't be using *that* plumber," I thought, deftly falling back to give him the room to sideswipe someone else, not me. But, while I most certainly did the right thing for my personal road safety, my thinking was not logical. ACME might really be the best plumbers in the county, but I anthropomorphized the driver and turned him into a company—a company I did not like and would not use.

The lessons? Make sure every company person and every bit of company collateral reflects the values of your business. Like it or not, faulty thinking or not, customer logic is a threat to be reckoned with.

Customer Chain of Experience—Delightful Journey or a Bad Trip?

Think about the customer chain of experience as his or her journey with your business. It starts with finding your phone number, then calling for an appointment. Next step? Finding the storefront or office, parking the car, walking inside, being greeted, and then shown where to go. The transaction is conducted and the customer drives away. Each step in the chain of experience defines you.

Recently, I stayed at a lovely hotel in New York. I put the address in my GPS and set off from the airport. I drove down the street that was listed but couldn't find a sign for the hotel. I ended up driving about five blocks, peering dangerously at buildings for a number that would orient me. Turns out I had passed the hotel. I found it on my second pass but all three parking spaces in front were taken. The hotel was not a small boutique (more than 200 rooms,) so I marveled at the dearth of parking places and rounded the block yet again. I had no luck on my third pass; it was snowing, and I could not see myself lugging my bags through the sleet from blocks away. There *has* to be a parking lot behind the hotel! Didn't there? Yes! I then expected prompt attention from a smartly uniformed valet. Nary a valet in sight! It took me three trips to get my stuff to reception. By that time, you could describe my mood like the weather . . . pissy. Not a positive way to start my journey with this hotel. What could have been done? Better signage—much better! Hire valets—lots of them! And, make the street address match the parking lot location.

Disney World gets this. Years ago, they profiled their average customer and found that most of them drove long distances and had small children. With the excitement of arriving at Disney, everyone jumped out of the car and ran to the park to enjoy their special day. The problem came at the end of the day. Leaving the park late at night while carrying cranky, crying, or sleeping children, many of these customers discovered their keys were not on them, and that they had been left in the ignition.

Disney understood that leaving on a negative note, even though their day had been wonderful, could put a damper on the whole experience. I can just hear an exhausted mother declaring, "That's it! We are *not* coming back!" How did Disney address this chronic problem? Well, they reasoned. Rather than have the customer wait perhaps hours for AAA to find them in the lot and let them into their car, Disney had locksmiths roaming the lot. These knights in shining armor helped the guest find their car, opened the door, and waved goodbye to the happy (and relieved) family within minutes. Brilliant! Ending the
customer experience on a positive is the last word in the journey. It is critically important. (Unfortunately, Disney was forced to discontinue this service.)

Sit down with your coworkers, and take the trip (in your minds) with your customer. Really examine the customer experience journey from start to finish. What if you got the perfect haircut from a talented stylist in a gorgeous salon with a fabulous front desk person. You left the building feeling great . . . and find a parking ticket on your car. A salon I frequent actually asks me where I parked and how much time is on the meter. When the time runs out, they offer to run out and feed the meter . . . because they don't want a parking ticket to ruin their great customer service—start to finish.

Or, maybe you've had the opposite happen. You wait far too long at the tire store for the front desk person to finish his phone conversation with his girlfriend. When he finally hangs up, he tells you to take a number before you even tell him what you want. But, you order the tires anyway (what else can you do?) and they are changed in mere minutes. You pay the front desk guy, and when you get in your car to drive away, the tech who changed your tires quickly hands you your keys, compliments your '95 Mustang, and wishes you safe travels! Sometimes, a bad front-end experience can be turned around with a great back-end one. *Everyone* in the organization can make or break your company. Start to finish.

So make a checklist:

- Is your phone number prominently displayed on your website?
- Is your website easy to navigate?
- Does your website come up first (or very close to first)?
- Do you have excellent signage?
- Is your parking lot clean? Do you have ample parking?
- Who is on your reception desk?
- How do you end the transaction?
- Do you escort customers out of the building?
- Have you asked them if they know their way out of your establishment?
- Do you offer parking validation?

Imagine every element. Between coming and going, a lot happens. For example, I don't like going to a Mexican restaurant (my fave) and seeing a long line of salsa drool down the menu. Yes, I drip my salsa off the chip too, but I wipe it off the menu. Not everyone does. Yuck!

Great food, disgusting restrooms? Would *you* go back? Does the manager walk to each table to ask if your meal was good? I had this happen recently and was told, "I would rather hear it from you now than read about it later." Smart! Every stop along the way defines the customer experience journey. Will it be memorable? Or will it be one they want to forget?

List EVERY step
of a customer's
chain of experience
for your business.

What can you do
to improve EACH step
of the experience?

Chapter 5

Secret to Success:
Passion or Career Contentment?

*"Choose a job you love and you never have
to work a day in your life."*
~ Confucius

*"Loathing Monday is a sad way to spend
one-seventh of your life."*
~ Mark Twain

Many of you reading this book love what you do. You went to college to get a degree and pursued your passion. Nursing, architecture, cosmetology, teaching, graphic arts, computer repair, animal care, food service . . . the list is long and varied. The stats, however, show that only one in three Americans love their job.

Some of you needed a job, and you took whatever you could get. You planned to stay there until you had time to look for something more fulfilling. Um, that was 20 years ago. You aren't happy, and guess what? We know it.

I had a woman come up to me at the close of a training I had done for her company. She waited until everyone left and shared with me that she hated her job. "No one knows." I looked her in the eye. "Really? I know." She stared, surprised. I continued, "I've watched you give me and everyone else the stink eye for the last four hours. It's not the secret you think it is." Her jaw dropped.

I told her she deserves to have a job she enjoys, and that her managers, co-workers, and customers all deserve to have a person filling her position who is happy. People who aren't happy can't offer good, genuine customer service.

Ever heard of "The Passion Trap"? Oddly, this theory tells us that not following your passion will make you happier. That people with a passion mindset focus on whether the job is right for them, and continually examine the minutiae of their work, asking "does it make me happy?" They often find it doesn't.

I disagree. I followed my passion, and mine is the best job in world! My passionate friends beg to differ, as they say their jobs are the best. We all love what we do, so it's a good argument—like having too many friends is a good problem.

Not everyone is passionate about their work. The best they can say is that they tolerate their work. What a terrible word! I "tolerate" getting a cavity filled. I "tolerate" sub-freezing weather. If you are merely "tolerating" your work, perhaps you can learn to love it. Try to be the best at the job you do and have pride in the service or product you offer. As Martin Luther King, Jr. said, *"If a man is called to be a street sweeper, he should sweep streets even as Michelangelo painted, or Beethoven composed music or Shakespeare wrote poetry. He should sweep streets so well that all the hosts of heaven and earth will pause to say, 'Here lived a great street sweeper who did his job well.'"*

In a *Fast Company* article about the mindset, Sebastian Klein wrote:

*"**ADOPT A CRAFTSMAN'S MINDSET**. The craftsman's mindset acknowledges that no matter what field you're in, success is always about quality. Once you're focused on the quality of the work you're doing now rather than whether or not it's right for you, you won't hesitate to do what is necessary to improve it."*

I was working with a company that makes food items. They're a really fun company with high morale and a quality product. One of the employees said to me, "It must be easier working with people in healthcare. My wife is a nurse, and she makes a difference every day. We don't." Well, he's right. Their food products aren't saving lives, or solving social injustice. But, there is something valuable about striving to continually improve what you make. Something wonderful about creating and sustaining a great working environment. Something priceless about cultivating friendship, respect, and teamwork. When people like coming to work, the world does change: one person at a time, one product at a time, one day at a time.

When I was a student at University of California, Santa Barbara, I worked for a semester in the admissions office. This was before computers, so we actually etched the class schedules in stone. Just kidding! We used paper. Yes, really!

We stuffed envelopes and sent the information out in the mail with a stamp on it. Imagine it. We stuffed envelopes for eight hours a day! It could have been enough to make a person think very bad thoughts about alternative uses for the letter openers we were given. Instead, we talked, laughed, and sang songs together. We had a blast!

Tim Peckham/hellotim.com

Yes, you *can* love what you do—even in the absence of your life's true passion. It's a choice you make . . . every day. Maybe you're not in your dream career (yet), but you can make your job fun and even meaningful. Food servers are some of the happiest people I know. And, yet most of them will tell you they're "only doing it until they get their screenplay sold, land that role in a Broadway play, or finish their degree in kinesiology." People who enjoy their jobs attract people who enjoy being your customers.

That said, there is great value in finding or reigniting the flame of passion. That's really the goal: finding a job you love because you love the purpose it serves. So, why not take responsibility for lighting the flame. Happiness neuro-science in a nutshell tells us we end up finding what we look for. So, seek care-fully. If your mantra is "I hate my job," odds are you will find examples all through the day to support that belief. Think what might happen if you switched to "I love my job"? If you can genuinely look for the good in what you do; if you start your work day believing it's going to be a great one, events *will* conspire to prove you right!

The secret to success is revealed at last. Enthusiasm is contagious. Passionate workers create passionate customers!

What is YOUR
favorite part of your
day to day responsibilities
at work?

Are there any
you would say
YOU are
passionate about?

What can YOU
do to make your job
more enjoyable?

Chapter 6

The Internal Customer

If you look after your internal customers,
you don't have to worry about
the external customers.
~ Richard Branson

When we think of our customers, we usually think of someone who enters our establishment or calls us from an outside line for an order or question. That's one kind of customer, the external customer. But you also have internal customers—those who rely on assistance from another department to fulfill their job duties. The way you treat each other internally is very often the same way you treat those who walk through the doors. Jan Carlzon, former President of Scandinavian Airlines, pointed out, *"If you're not serving the customer, your job is to be serving someone who is."*

Internal customers (staff members, fellow employees) play a key role in your business success.

If you're the order-taker at the window of a fast food restaurant, you better have a good relationship with the cooks, or guess who gets yelled at when

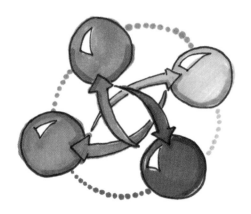

the order is wrong? If you're a physician and the phlebotomy department keeps patients waiting too long for their blood to be drawn, the customer's impression of you diminishes. To create a team with excellent internal customer service, all departments need to work together cooperatively. The key is regular inter-departmental meetings, a discussion of the expectations they have of each other, and the negotiation of a plan that makes everyone's job better.

Here's one I heard at one of my trainings. It's good. Good in a way that's fun to tell, but not so much fun for the stars of the story. John told us he stopped for lunch with two friends at a famous chain restaurant. You know, the one that serves breakfast all day and keeps pancake syrups on the tables at all times? As the hostess seated them, John and his friends noticed some ants climbing the wall and ending at the syrups. They politely pointed this out to the hostess. By the time their meals arrived, the brigade had tripled in size. Apparently, the ant lookout had sent an invitation to the rest of the army to join them at the BIG syrup party, and they'd accepted in droves. John pointed this out to their busboy, who said, "Well you didn't order breakfast; you aren't using the syrups. We'll get to it after you leave." John and his lunch-mates were dumbfounded.

So they ordered a side of extra ranch dressing and drowned the poor ants in a river of dressing. The hostess didn't care because she doesn't get tipped. The busboy didn't want to clean it up. The waitress was stiffed. This is not a team.

Need a happier story? Here's one. An anxious daughter arrived at a big-city hospital where her mother had just been taken as the result of a heart attack. She spent the day at her mother's bedside, advocating for more attentive care and unhappy with the service she wasn't getting. On her way out, the man at the parking kiosk asked, "Are you okay?" "Not really," she admitted. "My mom had a heart attack last night and it's been a long day." He told her he was sorry and advised her to first relax, and then get some rest. After an equally long second day, she encountered the same man at the kiosk and was impressed that he remembered her. "How is your mother?" he asked. The empathy and comfort shown by a nameless man at the parking kiosk had turned two very bad days into a positive experience. The moral of the story is: *everyone* is important; everyone can make a difference, especially if they feel like part of a team, a team that takes pride in its company. Here's how to cultivate the excellent team member, the excellent internal customer.

Encourage your staff to define their customer, to define what service quality means to them. Ask them to identify their goals around that, to discuss how they can better work together to meet those goals. Ask the members of a supporting department to define and better understand their roles in the big picture. Being taught to keep accurate notes is one thing; knowing those notes will be passed up the line and enhance the next step in the process creates team pride and increases the incentive to do stellar work.

Some ideas to create a team atmosphere:

- Communicate. Internal customer service can flourish only in environments where communication is valued, frequent, and thorough. Find ways to disseminate information so that all employees know what's going on; not just one department.
- Have fun off-site together so all employees can meet and bond. Have picnics and barbecues. Go out for comedy night, or a baseball game.
- Create kindness rituals.
- Say hello to everyone. I suggest companies practice the 10/5 rule. Within ten feet, acknowledge the person; within five feet say hello.
- Say "thank you." Sincerely, and often.
- Take personal responsibility. The one common denominator in every mess you find yourself in is *you*.
- Don't take things personally.
- Take problems to the right source.
- Don't gossip.

Employees who feel they are part of a passionate, connected team will deliver the excellent customer service the company strives for.

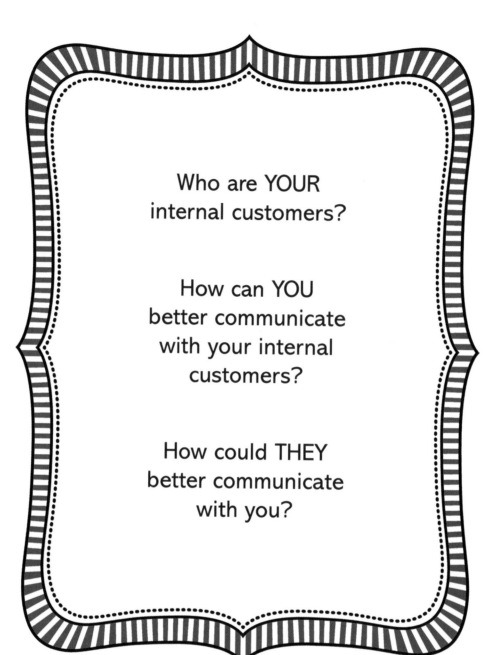

Who are YOUR
internal customers?

How can YOU
better communicate
with your internal
customers?

How could THEY
better communicate
with you?

Chapter 7

WHat CustomeRs WaNt

Your customers want what you want. Do you really need a lot of scientific research studies to identify what you, as a customer, want? I didn't think so.

Good customer service should be obvious. It used to be a given. Bad service used to be a rarity and was usually followed by "You're fired!" But in today's bleak business world where "I don't give a farmer's fart what you want!" is an all too common theme, what you want doesn't happen very often.

Let's visit a typical medium-end restaurant. Not fast food, but not mummified lychee nuts on whisper of apricot-glazed angel hair either. More like country-fried chicken meets homemade lamb stew. Your server doesn't notice you for five minutes. When she finally shows up with menus, she's a little too friendly (I don't like being called "folks" or "sweetheart") and doesn't know much about the specials. She is timely with the order but doesn't check back to see if I want an iced tea refill or dessert. And since when did servers get to sit down (or in some cases stand up) and eat in full view of the patrons, jumping up to see what you want with a half-eaten mouthful of spaghetti and meatballs? It seems that what used to be commonly expected good manners, courtesy, and service is so rare today that when it does happen, we find ourselves thinking "Wow. Now *that* was a nice touch!" or "This guy is getting a great tip!" A better research study than "What Do Customers Want?" would be "What the Heck Happened?"

I like feeling valued. When I'm a repeat customer, I love it when you remember my name and ask me if I want my usual diet soda with lemon. I like when people call when they say they will. When they empathize. When they aren't too chatty. I'm a great listener; I do it for a living, for Pete's sake. But I don't need to hear your life story while you're foil-wrapping my hair.

The nice thing about studying customer service is that it's kind of like studying ourselves. We know what we want. So at your next staff meeting, brainstorm about what you (as a customer) like, and don't

like. What makes you go back to the same business time after time?

Studies show that customers want . . .

- Reliability
- Responsiveness
- Assurance
- To Feel Valued
- Empathy
- Tangibles

Let's look at these individually.

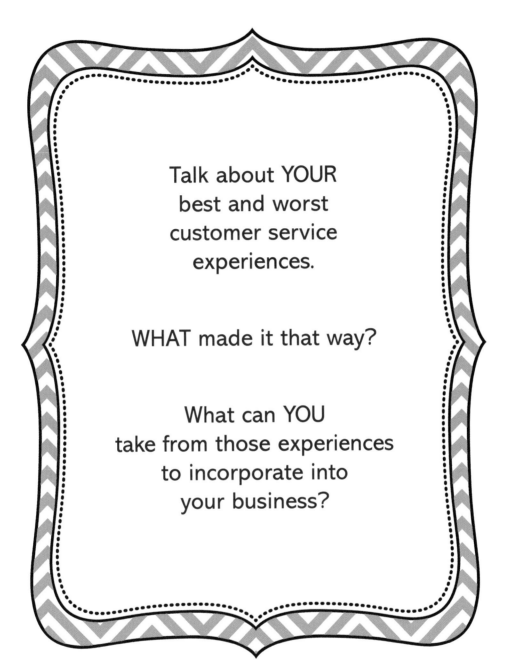

Talk about YOUR
best and worst
customer service
experiences.

WHAT made it that way?

What can YOU
take from those experiences
to incorporate into
your business?

Chapter 8

Reliability

There is nothing more heartbreaking in life than a broken promise. Behind every cheating spouse, every lying politician, every defrocked minister, every abandoned child, every Enron disaster, there lies the unmistakable fact of a broken promise. A promise to be faithful, to deliver the goods, to tell the truth, to love and protect, to honor your investment. Small wonder we have such skeptical customers these days.

Do you keep your service promise? Do you do what you say you will? Customers want the companies they do business with to be reliable. Reliable is defined as, "consistently good in quality or performance; able to be trusted."

Simply saying you have the best service is meaningless. Who claims their service sucks? No one. And yet, when I was searching for inspiring customer service quotes, I found several from the pen of a certain CEO whose company, *in my experience*, doesn't even try to *fake* good customer service. In this store, no one ever asks a customer if they need help. If that ever happened to me in this store, I'd be looking around for Rod Serling (Twilight Zone, you youngsters) or a hidden camera. Words without action mean nothing.

Does your company have a service promise? (If not, then create one! Make it short, honest, and powerful. It will be the guiding light for every member of your staff and will inform everything they do with its message).

"We got tired of beating around the bush."

Do you claim to:

- Give the best shop-ping experience pos-sible
- Treat customers with courtesy
- Respond promptly
- Offer the best prices
- Fully explain any questions the customer asks
- Keep you informed
- Offer convenience
- Want to know about and then fix any problems?

What is your business/service promise?

When I lived in Sacramento there was a restaurant (let's be clever and call it Restaurant X) that promised you could be in and out within 30 minutes or your meal was free. Here is a conversation at my office, "Where should we have lunch?" "I don't know, what sounds good?" "Well, I'm broke this week. Might as well go to Restaurant X so we can eat for free." Why? Because we *knew* that they would never be able to get us in and out on time. Corpo-rate had created a promise they could never deliver. The poor actual worker bees could never serve a lunchtime crowd in half an hour. They simply couldn't deliver the promise. That's a reputation you can live without. In fact, it's the worst kind of reputation. Inferior food, faulty products, sloppy service, even rudeness—all pale in comparison to the broken promise. *Ask yourself*: Are your processes aligned with your service promise?

Here's a magic formula for you:

Reliability = consistency + follow through.

It's as sturdy as E = mc squared! If I go to Del Posto's and have the Pumpkin Cappellacci, I want it to taste the same every time I eat there. I don't care if

different cooks make the same dish differently. I don't know what days the cook I like works, so please, keep it consistent. I like the Pumpkin Cappellacci at Del Posto's; that's why I go there!

I go to a certain local pathology lab because the techs are trained well. They do the procedures the same way every time. I don't get unnecessary needle pokes, and I'm not kept waiting longer than a few minutes. It's consistent. And I like that.

And what about the service rep who tells you there's a great deal going on for long distance, so you call back the next day and the new rep gives you a completely different price for the exact same product. Don't have one of your customer service reps tell me one thing and the next one tell me something different. If you have a policy, make sure *everyone* knows about it, and enforces it.

A famous women's clothing shop has a fabulous online presence. Great deals, good quality, cutting edge fashion. The problem? They are forever showing you clothes you can't buy! The savvy marketing person selects a great pair of pants, a sleek little black dress, or a classy pair of pumps and posts them on the home page. But poof! When the customer clicks on the item, it isn't available to purchase. Great for shopaholics who need to keep their spending in check. Bad for customers who really wanted it, so will go looking for something similar elsewhere (so they can actually purchase it)!

So to be reliable:

- Keep your service promise—do what you say you will.
- Under-promise and over-deliver. Don't tell me it will be a 15 minute wait when you know it will be more than an hour. Tell me two hours and if I agree to that, I'll be thrilled when you call me back in an hour!

Sometimes you just can't say yes. Customers will sometimes ask for the unreasonable, the impossible. Or they'll ask for something you've discontinued. Disappointment is sure to follow. You can't do anything about that, but you can do something to mitigate the disappointment. Come up with an offer that will leave them smiling instead of empty. My editor recently discovered an expensive gift she ordered at a discount from an online bookstore was not in stock. When Susan called to speak to someone about it, the rep couldn't deliver the item she wanted but he took the time to find something comparable and then offered to give her the same discount she'd been offered on the first one. She was delighted! And surprised.

"You can't promise your customer perfect weather, but you can hold an umbrella over them when it rains."

- Treat everyone the same, like you would your beloved grandmother. Do not let your prejudices color your approach. (Everyone has them; yes, even you!) An 18-year-old customer in a t-shirt buying gold jewelry should get the same respect as a 45-year-old businessman in a suit. A gang of Dead Heads deserves the same five-star service in a grand hotel as does the president of Chrysler Corporation.

"If you respect the customer as a human being, and truly honor their right to be treated fairly and honestly, everything else is much easier." ~ Doug Smith

What is YOUR
service promise?
If you don't
currently have one,
create one.

Are your
processes aligned
with YOUR
service promise?

Chapter 9

Responsiveness

Defined as "reacting quickly and positively," **responsiveness** has as much to do with timeliness as it does with answering requests and addressing frustra-

tions. A *Business Strategy Review* article describes customer responsiveness as *"accurately and insightfully giving customers what they need, want or don't yet know they want; and doing so more quickly than anyone else."* Many customers (myself included) won't call it excellent unless the response is fast, too. Are you hearing frequent complaints about the same issues? Better check your responsiveness meter.

Let's look at business hours, for example. The U.S. Postal Service and most banks are open Monday through Friday 8 am to 5 pm: when most people are working. Is that being responsive to their customers' needs? That you have to take time off work so you can mail your packages? Stand in line at the bank during your lunch hour? Some savvy banks (usually the small town, locally owned, kind) have expanded their hours to 7pm and Saturdays so we poor working stiffs can pick up a new check register (they don't have those at the ATM). Think about what your company is doing to invite people to walk through your doors. And what you could do to make it even better.

Here's one way to measure responsiveness: Think about which frustrations are most frequently voiced:

- "You are hard to find" or "I got lost trying to find you." Send a map to new customers. Or train your reps to offer directions on the phone.
- "Do you have a pen?" If they have to write something, have pens available! (I read about a company who offers "I ♥ Justin Bieber" pencils so customers won't take them. You gotta do what gotta do, right?)
- "Is there a place nearby to park where I don't have to put change in the meter?" Have directions handy, or even better, put out a bowl of quarters.

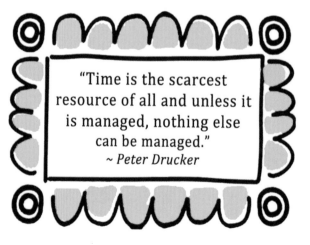

"Time is the scarcest resource of all and unless it is managed, nothing else can be managed."
~ Peter Drucker

Now evaluate how your company deals with timeliness.

What does "I'll get right back to you" really mean? If you tell me you'll call me right back, I wait by the phone; I assume it will be a few minutes. If you call me the next day, it will feel like next spring, and I will have called someone else by then. Be accurate and train your reps to be specific. If you know it could be a few hours, days, or weeks, tell me that! And keep me posted on your progress; don't keep me guessing. Second in line behind those who break promises is the time thief!

Our perception of timeliness has changed exponentially since the dawn of the digital age. When once we marveled that Swanson frozen dinners could present us with a full meal in an hour, now we stand impatiently in front of the microwave convinced it's the longest two minutes of our lives. We've gotten used to having everything done fast. Entire industries have grown up around getting it done faster. One-day dry cleaning. Eye glasses in an hour. In-N-Out Burger. Drive-thru Starbucks. ATMs. Same-day copying. Express delivery. In fact, a 2012 Oracle study found that customers expect responses to Facebook and Twitter inquiries within two hours. What?

Google is fond of saying that "fast is better than slow" and they strive to walk like they talk. *"We may be the only people in the world who can say our goal is to have people leave our website as quickly as possible."* Google is all about efficiency and speed. Good. A cumbersome, confusing site is not one I will visit.

Of course, sometimes customers have to wait. Think about how wait time is handled in your industry. Do you have a policy or promise within your organization? Do you need one? A customer kept waiting could turn into an online post that goes viral. Like this one:

WHEN CUSTOMERS MUST WAIT. . .

Dissatisfaction is often the result of uncertainty. Research shows that the most frustrating aspect of waiting is not knowing how long the wait will be.

The Psychology of Waiting:

1   *We have a natural fear of being forgotten.* Make eye contact occasionally with those in your waiting room. Tell them how long the wait will be. Give phone customers a call-back number directly to your desk.

2   *Unoccupied time feels longer than occupied time.* Do you have something to keep waiting customers busy? I watch TV almost never, so it's fun to watch Ellen while waiting to get my oil changed. About the *only* time I have to get caught up on "Brangelina" and the newest  king-to-be is, yep, the doctor's or dentist's office. Please have more than *Popular Mechanics* and *Parenting* or a dog-eared copy of *Time* from December 1992. Really?

3   *Perceived unfairness makes waiting seem longer.* We are not happy when someone who came after us is seated or brought into the exam room before us. Explain why we have to wait. I'll get it if I know the person who edged me out has a burst appendix, I really will!

"Waiting is good. It means you're not going to die. The person you need to feel sorry for is the one who gets rushed into the ER and treated first."

~ D. L., paramedic

4   *Anxiety makes the wait seem longer*. I need to be reminded that people get anxious in certain situations even when I don't. Maybe you've worked in a lab for years and think nothing of someone sucking your life's blood from your veins. You don't get nervous waiting. I do.

5   *Waiting alone is worse than waiting with one or more companions.*

6   *Any unexplained event or circumstance increases anxiety*. I have no idea what the codes being yelled over the loud speaker are. Gee, was that a bomb evacuation order? OMG, is there a shooter in the building? Maybe it's just a call for cleanup on aisle four. No one knows. Those codes just sound scary to me.

Dealing with irritated or nervous waiting customers is an important part of the responsiveness-timeliness element of your customer service program. When asked about wait times, one study showed that 49% of customers just want companies to show a willingness to improve. So are you willing?

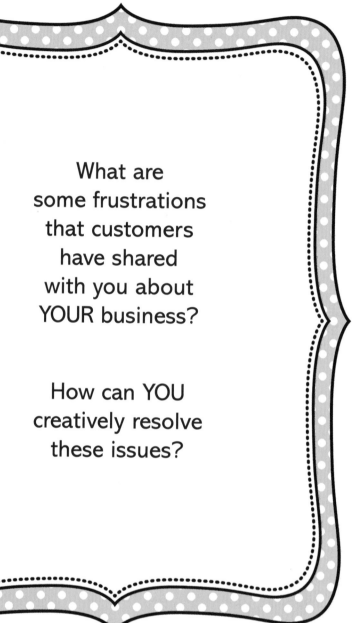

What are
some frustrations
that customers
have shared
with you about
YOUR business?

How can YOU
creatively resolve
these issues?

Chapter 10

Assurance and Trust

Fill in the blank:

"_____: the most trusted name in electronics."

"You're in good hands with _____"

"The most trusted name in news: _____"

[*Yes, the answers are at the end of this chapter.]

Companies pay big dollars to ad agencies to develop these slogans because they understand how important trust is.

Yahoo Finance writes: *"It's not uncommon for large American companies to spend billions on advertising annually to endear themselves into the hearts of the public and to prove that they are trustworthy. ... According to the 2013 Harris Poll Reputation Quotient, six out of ten U.S. consumers study a company's reputation before buying a product or service."*

Number one in the poll is Amazon, seen in 2013 as the most trusted company in the US—beating out Disney, Google, Johnson & Johnson and Apple. Robert Fronk, VP of Harris Interactive Reputation management says: *"There's no doubt that having an array of products and services at the right price is valuable. But they take that advantage and actually use a lot of the information that they're able to define about their consumers and make recommendations back to them, help them lead a better life, and even delight them on occasion."*

Does the name of your business call up a feeling of trust? Does your reputation support that? Do you live up to the expectations of your consumers?

According to a survey done by *Concerto Marketing Group and Research Now*, when customers trust a brand, 83% will recommend a trusted company to others and 82% will continue to use that brand on a regular basis. Your ability to earn customer trust is what will separate you from the competition. Here's how:

- **Keep your promises**. You might not remember, but they will. An article in *Psychology Today* reflects how broken promises can affect us personally. *"When we don't keep a promise to someone, it communicates to that person that we don't value him or her. We have chosen to put something else ahead of our commitment. Even when we break small promises, others learn that they cannot count on us. Tiny fissures develop in our relationships marked by broken promises."* And personally, *"Not keeping a promise is the same as disrespecting yourself. Ultimately it can harm our self-image, self-esteem, and our life."*

- **Be consistent**. I want to know I'll get the same service, the same product, the same expertise with every employee I encounter. I don't want to have to wait until Wednesday when Bob is working, because only he knows how to program my phone. I want everyone at my phone carrier to know how my phone works.

- **Pay outside vendors fairly and consistently company-wide**. Why? I once read an email sent to me by accident. (If she wasn't fired, this "accident" probably cost the sender a couple of sleepless nights.) In it, I discovered another speaker was being paid a significantly higher fee than I was. He was speaking at a smaller venue at the same conference where I was the keynote presenter. What I found exceptionally galling is that when I accepted the job, they told me they didn't have the money to pay my usual fee. They lied to me. I decided not to reveal my discovery, but I also decided never to work with that company again. Why? I don't trust them.

- *Never promise what you can't deliver.*
- *Don't try to hide your mistakes*. Trust is like a mirror: Once it's broken, you can never look at it the same again.
- *Never misrepresent what you are selling or providing*. Dr. Oz was called out for this in 2014 when Congress accused him of promoting snake oil products. He admitted that many of the products he endorses *"don't pass scientific muster."*
- *Don't badmouth other companies*. It's tempting to bash the competition but you just never know who you're talking to. One hospital CEO shared some stories with me about his cross-town rival hospital —whose CEO was my good friend! It wasn't gossip; it was his opinion. But his comments changed my feelings about him.
- *And while we are at it, don't gossip*. There is a Spanish proverb, *"Whoever gossips to you will gossip about you."* Enough said.

Trust is strengthened by the element of *assurance*, which is a two-sided thing: Giving assurance to your client or customer is one side; and behaving in a confident self-assured manner is the other. Both are important in building the trust we are looking for. Assurance defined: "a positive declaration intended to give confidence; a promise." And: "confidence in one's own abilities."

Are your customers dealing with a well-trained professional? Do you display both competence *and* confidence in your work? How does one do that exactly? What does competence / confidence look like? On a scale from 1 to 10, where do you fall on the skilled, qualified, specialist-in-your-field scale? Your peers? Your management?

I am a bright, well-educated woman. I know *nothing* about how my car runs, and I'm happy with that. If I wanted to dispel my belief that cars run on magic I would educate myself. But I have no desire to do that, so I have to buy cars that are reliable, keep them well-maintained, and find car mechanics who don't rip me off.

Years ago I was told I should always have my car maintenance done at the dealership. (I'm guessing a dealer told me that, but for a while, I believed it was good advice.) Not anymore. So upon moving to a new city, I took my Camry to the Toyota dealership for a checkup. "Do what you need to do," I said. (Don't smirk. I lean toward trust, remember?) When they called to tell me they were nearly finished, the mechanic said he felt he should tell me my automatic transmission fluid was dirty, but for a great price, he'd change it for me. "Fine," I said. Who wants dirty fluid? Not me! Then I thought about it. I know next to nothing about cars, but I did know that I had a manual shift.

Hmmm . . . So I called them and said, "I have a stick shift." "On a Camry?" he asked. "Yes," I replied. "I had to special order it." "Oh . . . well . . . then . . . never mind."

I truly believe that if I hadn't said anything, I would have been charged for an automatic trans-mission fluid change. And you know what happened? I no longer trusted them. And when I went to pick up my car, I asked to speak to the manager and he was busy. So that didn't make me happy. I continue to buy Camrys but I don't go to that dealer anymore. I drive a fair distance to someone I trust. Oh yeah, and I told everyone; I'm *still* telling everyone—in print!

The best compliment I ever get is when a client tells me they trust me. They trust me to offer a thought-provoking, educational, and uplifting training or keynote. They trust that I won't come with drama; that I'll always show up on time; that I'll not eat lobster and drink heavily on their dime. I communicate openly and often, which is one way to strengthen your relationships and build trust.

Trust is about honoring your word, your bond, your commitment—to your customers *and* to yourself. And that's called integrity.

*RCA, Allstate, CNN

What companies
do YOU trust?
Why?

Can you bring
any of THEIR
trustworthy
attributes to
YOUR business?

Chapter 11

Empathy

Empathy allows you to be professional and caring at the same time. Defined, empathy is the feeling that you understand and share another person's experiences and emotions; it's the ability to share someone else's feelings.

There is a difference between empathy and sympathy. According to Grammar Monster.com: *Empathy denotes the ability to understand and share the feelings of another. This ability usually derives from having shared the same, or a similar, experience. Sympathy denotes feelings of pity and sorrow for someone else's misfortune. This ability usually derives from having shared the same, or a similar, experience.* I think of it as the difference between acknowledging and understanding versus taking on another's pain. Sympathy can lead to burnout.

Michael Hess, in an article on *CBS Money Watch*, suggests the following questions:

- How does the person I'm trying to help feel?
- How would I feel if I were that person?
- No matter the request or the "rules," is there something I can/should do to help?
- What would I expect to be done for me if the roles were reversed?

- In the end, what would make this customer satisfied or (better yet) happy, and is there any reason I can't do it or find someone who can?

How do you show empathy? With . . .

- Body language
- Active listening
- Comforting language:
  ◦ "I understand…"
  ◦ "I see what you mean…"
  ◦ "I can see why you feel that way…"

It is really, really important to remind you:

1 **Don't fake it.** There is nothing worse, and nothing more transparent, than saying "I feel ya, buddy," when you don't. Well maybe there is, but a reputation for being phony is pretty damaging.

2 **Hire people who "get it."** You can't train someone to care, and if they don't care, genuine empathy is not in their repertoire—at all.

3 **Curb your enthusiasm.** If your customers know more about you than you know about them, that is not excellent customer relations. Telling your life story does not mean you are empathetic; it means you are narcissistic.

4 **Perhaps the most important of all: Don't tell someone you get "exactly" how they feel.** You don't. Even if you also lost a child, had a home fire, or missed a flight resulting in missing an important event, you don't know *exactly* how they feel.

Note: Some of you work in fields where compassion fatigue can set in. You have chosen to work in environments where heart-wrenching, emotional daily challenges are the norm. Here, empathy and/or sympathy can become overwhelming and can often lead to physical and emotional illness. A website titled "The Compassion Fatigue Awareness Project" offers free self-assessments, and ideas for moving toward wellness and self-care.

© A.BACALL

"Of course I'm listening to your expression of spiritual suffering.
Don't you see me making eye contact, striking an open posture,
leaning towards you and nodding empathetically?"

What is the difference
between empathy
and sympathy?

If you work in a place
where empathy
is a requirement,
what can YOU do to take
care of yourself to
avoid burnout?

How would you want
someone to express
empathy to YOU?
What phrases or gestures
would calm or comfort you?

Chapter 12

To Feel Valued

"**N**orm!" Remember that great group greeting whenever Norm, a TV character from the sitcom *Cheers!*, showed up at the bar? I think we all secretly envied Norm and the way his bar buds made him feel at the end of his workday. And the line from the show's theme song, "Where everybody knows your name," is really the theme for this chapter.

Not everyone wants to feel important. But we *do* want to feel that we matter. My friend shares her love of the Indian restaurant she frequents, not just for their superb Chicken Tikka Masala, but mostly because when she walks through the door, the owner beams "Hello, Susan! Would you like your usual table?" And when he offers her the menu, and then lowers his voice to tell her what's especially good that night, she feels like she's the only one he'll divulge that secret to—like Susan is his favorite customer of all time. Lovely.

As one of my all-time favorites, Maya Angelou, once said *"I've learned that people will forget what you said, people will forget what you did, but people will never forget how you made them feel."* Or as Damon Richards (perhaps not as well-known as Maya since I couldn't find one thing about him when I Googled him) says, *"Your customer doesn't care how much you know until they know how much you care."*

And if I leave your business feeling good, I will come back.

We've established that I am not now, nor will I ever be, an automotive whiz. At a shop I no longer do business with, I picked up my Camry after a routine oil change, and the mechanic said, "Next visit, we need to check the XYZ and replace the ABC." I replied, "Sounds good, can you put it on the computer so you can remember, since I won't." And when I came in for my next oil change, I reminded him that he said I needed some work done that he had made note of. "Look lady," he began. "I see 60 cars a day. I have no idea what you're talking about." Well, thank you! Way to make me feel special *and* stupid. The thing is, I know it isn't all about me (honest), but he *said* he would write it down. I *know* he sees lots of customers, which is why I asked him to make note of it! But telling me that made me feel small and insignificant. The guys at my new place are efficient, honest, and, most importantly, they act like I'm the only customer they've seen all day. I am royalty in that shop. (Admission: I bring them treats, which might help.)

How to make customers feel uniquely special?

Personalize the acknowledgment. I speak to the Orange County Community College District regularly. At my first gig there, I checked into the hotel to find a gorgeous bouquet of flowers waiting for me. I love flowers, and I must have let that slip during one of our initial conversations. And they remembered it. The gesture was kind, welcoming, and personal—it made me feel like they were excited to be working with me.

I don't like champagne, but I love the elegance of a fine champagne flute. Trust me: everything tastes better in an elegant glass. One year I spoke for a group at Pacific Gas & Electric and mentioned this particular fondness. A year later, on a return engagement, not one but two people brought me my water in a beautiful champagne flute. Wow. They listened . . . they remembered . . . I mattered!

Anticipating needs is another way to make a person feel special. Does your dentist offer you earbuds and a choice of music for a long procedure? Does your hotel concierge offer you a wake-up call? Does your accountant offer you coffee and cookies while you wait for the bad (or good) news? Does your yoga instructor welcome you back with a warm greeting and extra attention in class when you've been gone a few weeks? Does your dental office remember you need antibiotics before a procedure and call it in to the pharmacy _and_ remind you?

A resident at a retirement community once complained bitterly to the marketing rep about how neglected he felt because no one ever walked the dining room anymore to fill them in on the latest company hires and plans. He felt totally disconnected from his own home. The rep not only heard him but wrote a heartfelt, respectful letter thanking him for having the courage to speak up and for making her a better liaison. He now thinks she walks on water and tells all new prospects what a great place it is.

Offer exclusive deals. Discount coupons are a bit ho-hum when you can find them in your Sunday paper. The owner of a restaurant I'm in at least twice a month refused to let me pay one evening (we were a party of four that night) because he values my patronage and it was his way of saying thanks for the hundreds of times he'd seen me. That beat a coupon by a country mile. My yard guy once pulled out a dead section of my hedge and replaced it with a matching new green one without being asked. I told everyone in my neighborhood. I've had a cell company rep offer to get my monthly bill lowered, and this was when I went in for something else entirely. I nearly dropped to the floor. My friend shared a great story of a dress shop she frequents (and spends a lot of money in) once offering, not only to find and order the party dress she wanted in her size, but to alter when it arrived. The sales gal even popped the perfect scarf inside her bag, gratis. What original, personalized things or exclusive deals can *you* offer?

Get feedback. Ask your customers for their ideas and concerns. Ask them what works and what doesn't? A generic survey is one thing, but if I'm a regular customer, take the time to ask me what I think about your website, specials, uniforms, logo, or signage. Nothing says "I respect and value your opinion" more than asking for their input.

Remember names. A person's name is *"the sweetest, most important sound in any language,"* writes Dale Carnegie in his classic book *How to Win Friends and Influence People*. We feel valued and respected when someone remembers our name. In conversation, we feel more engaged when someone uses our name. In business, using someone's name can influence the way a customer feels about you and your brand.

What's in a Name?

- Make the effort to use the right name and pronounce it correctly. Don't force people to constantly correct you: "It's Terese, not

Theresa." Or "It's Baumgarten, not Bumgarten." So annoying. Using names and pronouncing them correctly can set you apart.

- Ask customers how they prefer to be addressed. "Hi, I'm Jean," I'll say to meeting attendees at trainings, "and you are . . .?" To which I sometimes hear: "My name is Dr. Doright." Whoa, jump back Jack, now *I know* you're a doctor! My point is, don't assume (which I often do) that someone wants you to use their first name. Start with their title and surname and go to first names only if you're invited to.

Treat each customer as your best one, learn their names, ask for their opinions, and find unique, personalized ways to appreciate them. Valued customers are loyal customers.

Off the top of
your head,
can YOU recite the
first and last name
of five of your customers?

Can your employees?

How can YOU
better anticipate
the needs
of your customers?

Chapter 13

Tangibles

"*If they can see it, walk on it, hold it, hear it, step in it, smell it, carry it, step over it, touch it, use it, even taste it; if they can feel it or sense it, it's customer service.*" So says the Super America Training Program.

We're talking tangibles.

Examples:

- The food was smackalicious at the trendy new restaurant, but your wine glass had a lipstick print on it. Not yours.
- Someone dumped their kid's dirty diaper on the ground in the parking lot of a retail store and you almost step in it getting out of your car. You look around: trash all over.
- The medical assistant who is taking your blood pressure has breath that would stop a train.
- You are filling out a form and you ask the receptionist for a pen. She hands you one—with a chewed-on cap.
- You open the door to the bank and it's covered with sticky fingerprints.
- You are handed a business card and notice his dirty fingernails.

- Oh look! A fish tank in the dentist's office. Only . . . the fish are dead (a sad but true story). And when the receptionist scooped them up and walked away, I heard a toilet flush in the distance.

We notice the tangibles before we enter your doors; and we continue to note them until we drive away.

I don't have the expertise to evaluate my medical care. But I do notice that your receptionist used way too much perfume this morning; and there's a quarter-inch of dust on the baseboards in your examining room. Well? You always make me wait in there with my backside exposed to the wind, so what else am I to do with the time?

If your customers are talking about *anything* but the attention they get or the products you sell, you have a problem.

That bank in the list? The one with the fingerprints on the door? When I told the teller, she informed me the staff uses a different door to enter the workplace so they never see the front door. How about tracing the route of the typical customer on a daily basis, before the bank opens, to see what it looks like from *their* vantage point?

Fair or not, we really do judge books by their covers. It's that first impression thing. It takes just seven to 17 seconds at first meeting to form an opinion. There isn't time to notice your sparkling personality. It's your appearance we see first. So please . . .

Take Pride In Your Appearance

Office attire. Business dress. Dress appropriately. These vague phrases leave room for interpretation the size of the black hole. "Appropriate" has a loooong continuum. An office manager once told me about his new-hire for the front desk. She had a good résumé, excellent references, and a sunny attitude. She showed up for her first day with

nice, round-toed pumps, a cute pencil skirt just below her knees, with a matching sleeveless top. And about an inch of her belly was showing. It was a crop-top. Appropriate? To her, it was. You have to be specific.

I know a company that caters to high-end (read wealthy, well-heeled) clients. They have a list of dressing dos and don'ts that would make even Anna Wintour weep. The list addresses everything from fingernails (length, shape, color) to men's facial hair regulations. It forbids perfumes of any sort, limits piercings to one in each ear for women, and more. It leaves no doubt about what is expected. And that's a good thing! Sure takes the guesswork out of getting dressed for work, right? More importantly, the client sees a staff attired in a tidy, predictable, uniform manner. Boring perhaps, but it is what they expect. It puts them at ease. It cultivates trust.

Remember when the winning women's lacrosse team went to the White House in 2005? There was this big controversy. It was over their attire. Some of the young women wore flip-flops. It was perceived as disrespectful; casual to a lethal degree. And so their footwear (or lack thereof) overshadowed their national championship win. Again, fair or not, attention to attire is as important as good manners.

The New Rules

Americans spent $1.65 billion last year on tattooing. Forty-five million Americans sport at least one tattoo. Yet many companies still do not have policies regarding this art form / body wear. For some companies, it's a non-issue. For others, it has become a pretty big deal. It's a personal-freedom versus company-policy controversy that mostly goes unaddressed in any kind of formal way.

I work a lot in long-term care, and I've met only a handful of HR professionals in that field who have addressed the tattoo issue. Right or wrong, the elderly (with some happy exceptions) are not yet accustomed to full-sleeve tattoos. They are frightened by them. Great customer service means not scaring those you serve. Companies who fix computers can afford to be more relaxed about their tattooed techies. So develop a policy that makes sense for you, make sure everyone knows about it, and stick with it. Enforce it across the board.

Belly shirts, 6-inch purple patent leather heels, and holey jeans are still considered inappropriate for the workplace. I once did a customer service training for a water distribution company. They allow jeans in the office but request that they be "nice." One Monday, the young woman who drives the delivery truck showed up in a pair of jeans that had set her back $258. They had frayed hems and holes in the knees. Well, *she* thought they were nice. See what I mean about being specific?

What about aroma? Is that a tangible? Um, yeah. When I turned 40 my eyesight went. Like that day. So I had to get glasses. If you don't wear glasses, what you might not know is that once your glasses are ordered and they arrive, the optometrist then fits the frames to your face. So I sit at a small, narrow table; he sits across from me and I put them on. Then he raises his arms and reaches out to adjust the frames to my face.

I stop breathing. His body odor is shockingly, disturbingly bad. He adjusts the frames and asks if they're ok. They aren't. But I mumble "just fine" and nearly stagger out the door.

I returned later in the week when I was sure he was not on duty and asked his assistant to adjust the frames so I could actually see (which was my goal). "Why didn't you have them adjusted when you came in and picked them up?" she asked. With just a little snotty tone in that query.

"Well to be truthful," I said, "the man who was helping me smelled really bad."

"Yeah, we hear that a lot," she admitted.

What? It wasn't like I said he had four eyes so I couldn't bear to look at him.

There's not much you can do about having four eyes. But body odor? He can shower, use deodorant, wash his clothes more often. Or go to a doctor to see what's up. It was that bad.

Then she added (which was both inappropriate and awesome at the same time):

"His wife smells just as bad as he does."

Oh good to know. If it's a family affliction then I'm okay with it? I won't ever go back there again.

How about décor? That's a tangible rife with improvement potential!

- Water and tend to your plants, or buy fake ones. Dead plants worry me. If you can't keep your plants alive I get concerned for my own welfare.
- Get rid of out-dated, dog-eared magazines.
- Offer new pens and crisp clean paper to work with.
- Clean your office chairs. Soiled chairs have a worry all their own. As in: Is that a coffee stain there? Or . . . um, something else?
- Keep anything made of glass sparkling clean.
- Hire people to keep parking lots and grounds free of detritus.

I was training at a hospital with lovely, well-manicured grounds. When I walked to the training center the first day, I noticed an empty box of Red Vines sitting on the grass. My auto-response was to pick it up and dispose of it. In mid-reach I thought nope. This training is on customer service, so let's see if someone else picks it up. Five days later, *it was still sitting on the grass*. Later, in session, I asked them if they'd seen a Red Vines box on the lawn. All 100 of them had. Why had no one picked it up? You guessed it: "It's not my job." Really? It wasn't about pulling weeds or mowing the entire expanse of lawn. It was about taking three seconds to pick up a piece of trash. Train your staff to take ownership of the company they work for. Remind them it *is* their job to do whatever it takes to ensure that all your tangibles are what they would want to see, hear, feel, taste, and smell. Make a list of the tangibles in your place of business and empower *everyone* to be responsible for them.

What tangibles
may a customer encounter
on a visit to YOUR
company parking lot
or lobby?

How often do YOU
walk through the
"customer path"
in your building?
Your employees?
What do you see?
What can you improve?

Chapter 14

Above and Beyond:
The New Normal

Imagine: Your mother has just died. There are a million things to do and it's hard to be efficient while you are half-drowning in waves of grief. You notice a pair of shoes you need to return, but it's so not a priority. You haven't even written the obituary yet. So you email the company to say you'll be late returning them, and why. Next day, in the midst of writing the list of invitees to the funeral, a UPS man rings the doorbell. He's there to pick up your shoes . . . and he's got a beautiful basket of flowers. "Zappo's is very sorry for your loss, ma'am."

Now *that's* above and beyond.

Your customers can always go one block over and get the same product; and the online competition is only a mouse-click away. Making customers feel special, being helpful even if there is no immediate profit in it, surprising them beyond their expectations—these are the things that engender loyalty. It's going from good to *great* customer service.

Zappo's empowers their employees to do the unexpected, to anticipate their customers' needs and meet them in an imaginative way. They have a company culture that encourages staff to exceed expectations. They don't track how long they stay on the phone with each customer; they trust them to know how much time it will take to give each person an optimal experience. Want to know more? Read Zappo's CEO Tony Hsieh's book *Delivering Happiness*. The title alone is worth the read, but it really does deliver unique, why-didn't-I-think-of-that ideas, truly inspired tips, and the kind of motivation that will change your company from the inside out.

Mostly taken from the restaurant/hotel industry where the competition is especially fierce, here are some of my favorite stories:

Worried sick about her 89-year-old dad who lived in a town that was expecting a national disaster-sized storm, a woman called the local Trader Joe's. She wanted to be sure he'd have access to food during the deluge and asked if Trader Joe's offers a delivery service. "No," said the voice on the phone. "I'm afraid we don't." Exhausted and emotional, she explained the reason. "Oh! Then we'd be happy to," came the welcome reply. "What's his address?" And here's the *above* the above-and-beyond part: They didn't charge for the groceries.

LaFonda Hotel in Avila Beach has a little minibar/goodie basket in each room. No price list attached. Why? It's free. Yep, all of it. (Haven't we all been stunned

to see how much a bag of chips and a bottle of water can cost when it comes from one of those stupid little fridges?) Suddenly, my sweet little getaway weekend just got that much sweeter.

The famous pink hotel in our town, Madonna Inn, serves rock candy crystal sugar sticks with their iced tea. Such a simple touch, but it makes me happy.

And speaking of pink, I love that single pink rose I receive when I get my annual mammogram.

Just for fun, a Hampton Inn customer once wrote in the "additional comments" section of his online reservation form that he'd like a framed photo of Alfonso Ribeiro on his nightstand. When he arrived and entered his room, he saw this. Clever, creative, and so much fun. I'm guessing he did a "Carlton" happy dance right then and there. Think he'll book Hampton again? Think he'll tell about a million people?

My friend stayed at a hotel in Hawaii where they had an employee who would wander the pool and beach areas offering to spray-clean the suntan oil and sweat off guests' sunglasses. And, at the height of the day's heat, they gave out complimentary popsicles. It's the little things, right?

A Japanese custom called Oshibori offers hot hand towels in the winter, and cold ones in the summer for dining customers. Some airlines also offer these to first class flyers. Sometimes the towels are infused with aromatherapy. Two tangibles in one. Above . . . and beyond heavenly.

At the Renaissance Hotel in Seattle, patrons seated for breakfast are served a complimentary breakfast goodie. A little smoothie one day; a fresh blueberry yogurt treat the next. Call it an amuse-bouche for the breakfast crowd. Utterly charming.

At the Hyatt Beaver Creek in Vail, Colorado, management offers complimentary boxes of s'more makings for their evening bonfire. They included *everything*—from marshmallows to skewers. Brilliant.

Anticipating Needs

On the way to above-and-beyond are the willingness and the talent to identify, anticipate, and then meet your customers' needs.

Carmine Gallo wrote an excellent article in *Forbes* about anticipating customer needs. While staying at The Grand Del Mar, a five-star resort, he was continually impressed with the staff, who had achieved greatness in the area of anticipating his needs. He writes:

"I asked the person why everyone seems to anticipate the needs of a guest. 'It makes us stand out,' he said. The employee was exactly right. The reason why this level of service leaves a positive impression—and why you, as a leader, must coach to it—is because it happens so infrequently that customers will pay a premium for it. I've studied the best brands in the area of customer service and all of them train employees to anticipate unexpressed wishes. It's a key component to an exceptional customer experience."

The San Diego Westin has five ice water containers in its lobby, with such delicious additions as pineapple, honeydew, orange, and grapefruit. And plain for the purist, of course. I've also seen fresh apples or granola bars in a bowl at the registration counters of some hotels. And the Double Tree Inn offers warm chocolate chip cookies at check-in. These places anticipate I'll be parched and hungry after my long trip. Their consideration of my needs does what Gallo is talking about: it sets them apart.

The hospitality industry has it easy in the search for ways to go above-and-beyond. It's their *business* to serve, to pamper, to pay attention to their guests. If you own a plant that makes gearshift knobs, or maybe you run a tax service, you'll have to work a little harder to come up with things. (My accountant friend sends her clients a quarterly newsletter with helpful tips and reminders that really help at tax time. AND she has a cappuccino bar in her office for her personal meetings with clients.) Ask yourself what might make your own experience better and the answers will come.

Harvard Business Review writes: *"There's only one way to create emotional connections with customers: by ensuring every interaction is geared to delighting them. That takes*

more than great products and services—it takes motivated, empowered front-line employees." And the piece goes on to suggest that *"Giving frontline employees responsibility and autonomy inspires them to do whatever they can to improve the customer experience."*

Brainstorm, strategize, and train to the above-and-beyond mission. Make it an expectation you have for every employee. Soon, it'll be second nature to them. Why? Because it's fun! Employees *enjoy* saying "yes!" They *like* making others feel good! Soon they'll be coming up with their own unique practices. Kindness begets kindness. It's true!

Brainstorm ideas
for your business to go
above and beyond
what you, and perhaps
similar companies to yours,
currently offer.

Brainstorm means go crazy
with ideas, throw them out,
don't judge them until you
are done. Sometimes the
wilder the better.
Then when done go
through and discuss what is
feasible . . . or not.

Chapter 15

The All-Important First Impression

*You never get a second chance
to make a first impression.
~ Head & Shoulders shampoo*

A first impression is quick, powerful, and lasting. People form opinions of others fast, often with only minimal information. And they weigh that initial information much more heavily than later information. People believe the first things they learn are the "truth."

Research shows that 55% of a person's opinion is determined by physical appearance. (No, appearances *shouldn't* matter that much, but the numbers don't lie. Appearances do matter—a lot). The remaining 45% is body language, demeanor, and mannerisms. Sunnafrank's "predicted outcome value theory" holds that we predict the future of a relationship as soon as we begin communicating with another person.

What's more, we really don't get a chance to remedy a bad first impression;

that customer simply won't come back. Suffice it to say—first impressions in customer service are critical.

First impressions matter when you want to build a lasting trust. You often have just *one chance* with a new customer. I might not remember your name, but I

will remember you had a greenie stuck in your teeth. First impressions can be almost impossible to reverse. They set the tone for the whole company, and for the upcoming customer experience with that company. *Psychology Today* says: *"The exaggerated impact of first impressions is related to the halo effect, that phenomenon whereby the perception of positive qualities in one thing or part gives rise to the perception of similar qualities in related things or in the whole."*

Things to consider:

- It starts with your online presence—your website. According to researchers at the Missouri University of Science and Technology it takes less than two-tenths of a second for an online visitor to form a first opinion of your brand once they've perused your company's website. They asked participants to scan the websites for 20 seconds and were able to track eye movement. Ask yourself what three things you want visitors to do as a result of viewing your site. (If one of those is "contact us," then I advise you to make your contact information easy to find. It drives me crazy when it's buried in the convoluted depths of the website!)
- Positive opening statement. When I walk through your door, don't bond with me by complaining about the heat, or how tired you are, or how busy it's been. Project a positive attitude. Make me happy that I came in.
- What are the first impressions at your workplace? Invite your staff members to make a list. You'll be startled to find how different they are.

- If you are a business that takes appointments, please be on time. I don't care if traffic is bad, or if your last customer talked your ear off. Allow for delays. And don't double book.

- Be authentic. Authenticity is the true heart of customer service. One of the best compliments I've ever received came from Martin Gamez with the Center for Employment Training—one of my favorite groups to work with. He wrote:

  > *"What makes Jean so genuine is that she is the same person offstage as she is onstage. No bait and switch here!"*

First impressions are not about "fake it till you make it." Be real. The owner of a hotel told me about Greg, her front desk clerk, who greeted everyone this way: "Hey, how's it goin'?" Everyone. Every customer, every time. It sounded fake, because it was.

- **Be Comfortable**. If you are uncomfortable, the customer will be too. I do not enjoy getting my blood drawn. At one place, the phlebotomist seemed very nervous, which did not inspire my confidence in him. I thought it might be a good idea to admit to him I was nervous. Know what he said? "Not as nervous as I am." Yeah, I asked for another phlebotomist.

- **Physical Appearance**. Is your appearance giving the right impression? Yes, I know the current fashions include bare legs, crop tops, and lots of bangles. But if you work in a retirement community (where the customer is elderly), choose closed-toe pumps, wear stockings and tailored dresses, and keep the jewelry to a tasteful minimum. It's what they expect.

- **Smile**. So important there's a separate chapter on it. Put the time and energy into selecting front-line staff who naturally exude the warmth and professional image you want for your business. Hire for these qualities and then train them well. Offer regular "tune-ups" (refresher trainings and workshops) to ensure these great employees stay that way, offering impeccable and consistent customer service with every person, every day.

- **The Handshake**. Short and sweet, the handshake is often overlooked. But its impact is large. A bad handshake can have a subliminal effect, tainting the customer's entire opinion of you. Am I exaggerating?

The University of Iowa found that those people who start job interviews with a firm, strong handshake are always perceived in a more favorable light than those who shake hands like a limp fish. Interviewers perceived students with good handshakes as being more outgoing, with better interpersonal skills.

Business Insider says: *"The perfect handshake is a smooth, swift, and confident raising of your hand, which is placed firmly in the palm of your connection's hand. It requires that you look that person in the eyes, hold a firm, but not too tight grip, and smile. Stifle your nerves and give a genuine smile with your eyes. When you smile you put the other person at ease, they smile, and you can both relax."*

My friend Rich worked at a place where they had a large mirror installed at the employee entrance with the words, "WHAT DO OUR CUSTOMERS SEE?" emblazoned on it.

I ask you: What do *your* customers see?

Start looking
at your on-line presence.
Then do a complete
walk through,
starting from the
parking lot,
to look at your business
through your
customer's eyes.

Chapter 16

The Lost Art of Listening

"*The most basic of all human needs is the need to understand and be understood. The best way to understand people is to listen to them,*" says listening guru Dr. Ralph Nichols. We'll be spending some time with this topic so quit fidgeting and listen. Because when it comes to great service, there is no better way to demonstrate that you care, that you want to understand, than listening, *really* listening to the customer. Listening has two purposes: Sure, we listen to get information: but listening also bears witness to another's expression, acknowledging and affirming them.

And here's a wellness bonus: Listening also helps make life easier in general. Good listening skills help you with stress management, make you a more assertive communicator, and help you become a better leader.

Listening is our most frequently used and *least studied* communication skill. Odd, because excellent listening skills can separate the decent sales person from the stellar one, or elevate the mediocre manager to a superstar, even distinguish the good friend from the best-friend-forever kind.

After a long career in business, Peter Nulty had this to say about listening, "*Of all the skills of leadership, listening is the most valuable —and one of the least understood. Most captains of industry listen only sometimes, and they remain ordinary leaders. But a few, the great ones, never stop listening. That's how they get word before anyone else of unseen problems and opportunities."*

Have you ever been busted for not listening? Have you been told you're "an amazing listener?" Do you *believe* you're a superior listener? Yep, I know you think you are. Just like most people think they're good drivers. The truth is, a great many of us are not. So listen up.

Here are my first three reminders for listening:

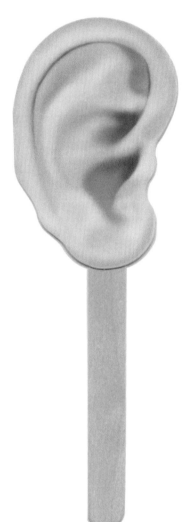

- Remember, listening hard, listening well is *a choice*. You do not have bad listening skills in your DNA (nice try, though).
- Listening is *not* simply being quiet, waiting for your turn to talk. A little thing called the "rebuttal tendency" (developing your counter-argument while the speaker is still speaking) happens when you are not actively listening but simply waiting your turn.
- Listen *all the way to the end.* Don't assume. I have heard 30-year veteran receptionists say, "I don't need to listen to the end. I can tell what they want within ten seconds of them starting to talk." Umm . . . no. That kind of arrogance can get you into so much trouble!

The statistics around listening are a little frightening as well as fascinating. Basically (no surprise) we don't seem to be very good at it.

- 75% of the words that go through our ears are ignored, misunderstood or forgotten.
- Our attention spans are short. Most of us listen for about 17 seconds at a time.
- We listen to people at a rate of 125-250 words per minute, but we think at 1,000-3,000 words per minute.
- Less than 2% of people have had any formal education on how to listen. (Yes, you can learn to be a better listener. I teach a session on listening skills every year to the wonderful people at California Agricultural Leadership program. They understand that listening is critical to good management.)
- Images go into your long-term memory, whereas words live in your short-term memory.
- In a linear one-way listening task, when presented with a list of words, people can remember, on average, seven items. (I feel better when wait staff write down what I want. Not when they say, "Don't worry, I'll remember.")

So how does this affect customer service? First and foremost, it helps us to really *focus* on what the customer is saying. Listening gives us . . .

- Insight
- Context
- A different perspective
- A demonstration of respect

Furthermore, despite your best efforts to conceal your disinterest, people know when you are *not* listening. It shows non-verbally—in your lack of eye contact, fidgeting, looking at your watch, or a deadpan expression.

In the field of healthcare, studies reveal that:

- Physicians interrupt 69% of patient interviews within 18 seconds of the patient beginning to speak. As a result,
  - In 77% of the interviews, the patient's true reason for visiting was never elicited!

- ○ Patients are less likely to sue practitioners with good bedside manners (with good listening being at the top of that list).
- ○ Effective listening is a significant predictor for patient satisfaction.

Apply these results to your own line of work and you'll be surprised to find how valuable they are to fostering a culture of laudable listening talents.

And finally, the following noteworthy aside on gender and listening is well worth a listen. In fact, entire books have been devoted to this issue (remember John Gray's *Men are From Mars, Women are From Venus?*).

Men and women listen differently; they employ different listening styles. (Hope you were sitting down for that. Pretty shocking, I know.) When listening, women make more noises such as "mm-hmm" and "uh-huh," while men tend to listen silently, interjecting sparsely and usually only to ask for clarification. This difference in response style can cause women to feel unheard, while men tend to think that women "over listen."

It's a proven fact: When a male speaks, he is listened to more carefully than is a female speaker, even when she makes the identical presentation. And we females are not exempt from this egregious gender bigotry: Even when women listen to other women, females recall information more accurately from a male speaker than from a female one.

Here's more:

As young as five years old, females are more sensitive to a range of tones than men. Women's comfort levels are lower than that of men. And men tolerate significantly louder background noises than women.

Men, on average, lean toward linear thinking, while women are more circular. When this is not recognized and people are in different modes, the conversation can go off the rails quickly. Linear thinking is logical, focused, objective, disciplined, and goal oriented. Circular thinkers go from idea to idea, rooted in a drive to be inclusive and transparent—a belief that the answer will come when everyone with an interest is present and a diverse array of thoughts are considered. When I am asked how my weekend was, don't expect a one word reply like "good." Expect details. Just sayin'.

In an article wonderfully titled *Men are Like Waffles; Women are Like Spaghetti,* the author sums up male/female communication this way: Men don't know how to listen to women, and women don't know how to talk to men. Now discuss.

And finally, there is a big difference between being quiet and really taking interest. Don't judge, just listen.

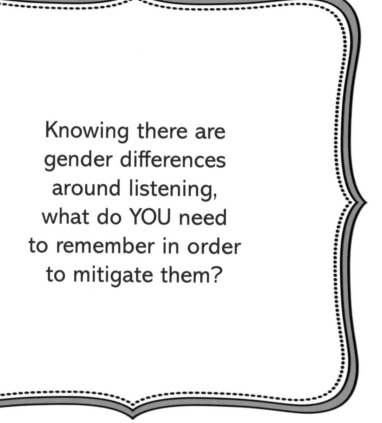

Knowing there are
gender differences
around listening,
what do YOU need
to remember in order
to mitigate them?

Chapter 17

Barriers to Listening

Picture this: You've just purchased a $4000 TV at one of those big box stores. The place is awash in hurried holiday shoppers, holiday music plays in the background (annoyingly hoping you are "rockin' around the Christmas tree"), and the checker is calling for help on the store's intercom. He asks you something unintelligible, but you think it has something to do with an important component of your new TV. You really want to answer correctly so you don't end up spending hours setting up the TV only to find you are missing the power cord! You tell him you didn't quite get that and ask him to repeat the question. To which he replies . . . "What?" You, the customer, *and* your fellow customers (you can hear them sighing impatiently behind you, can't you?), are not happy. So many barriers to listening and hearing; so little understanding.

For your consideration, here are a few of them:

Emotional and mental filters. Like it or not, we all have preconceived ideas, feelings, hidden agendas, and prejudices. Adding insult to injury, sometimes we assume bias on the speaker's part and predict what they will say before they say it. You've heard of "contempt prior to investigation?" Well, this is known as "stupidity leading to super-bad consequences." Prejudice can apply to myriad issues beyond the usual race, religion, or politics. These can range from age to accent, gender to gym choice, appearance to education, language skills to laughing style. The defensive phrase "But I've dealt with people just like them," actually emphasizes your subconscious prejudice. Effective listening means being open to the ideas and opinions of others—without judgment. Effective listening does not equal agreement with the speaker's ideas; it does mean you are willing to listen, willing to understand their point of view.

The Folly of Multi-tasking. From job requirements to personal point of pride, the talent for multi-tasking is touted often. Where listening is concerned, however, I'm not a fan. Maybe *you* can check your phone and listen to me, but I don't believe you.

Twice, I went to lunch with the general manager of a company who had hired me to do some workshops. I really liked him and found it puzzling that his staff reported such negative interactions with him. Not surprisingly, this company suffered from low morale, high turnover, and a reputation for poor customer service. His staff just didn't care, but I was "on the case." On my first day, I met with Mr. GM in his office. His desk was facing the door, his computer on a console behind it. On seeing me, he jumped up, came over and gave me a professionally appropriate (no touching below the waist) hug. Good start.

Then he sat down, swung his chair around to face his computer, and said, "Go ahead, I'm listening, I just need to finish checking emails." My response? "John, this is one of the reasons they hate you." John was a busy person and profoundly Type A. Not a bad guy—in fact, a good guy. He just didn't understand that having his back to me was rude and disrespectful; it showed me he wasn't really listening. I imagine the only reason he didn't check his phone continually during lunch is because we didn't have smart phones back then.

So it works both ways: If you're checking your phone, your customer is not being heard. And if your customer is checking his phone, *you* are not being heard. Modern technology is great but it has its downside. I used to be able to detect whether my students were listening to me or not by their body language. With today's laptops, tablets, and iPads, I can't tell if they're taking notes or checking out who un-friended them on Facebook!

Personal distractions. Many listening barriers are highly individual, unique to you. They can include:

- Thought detours—or getting derailed by something the speaker has said. For example, you own a carpet cleaning business and your new customer is telling you about a red wine stain. You suddenly remember you need to pick up some Merlot for your dinner guests tonight. And darn, what else do I need at the Bev-Mo?

- Disinterest or boredom.
- Distractions or being preoccupied. Yes, it's hard to concentrate when you are stressed about the biopsy you were ordered to have last week. Maybe this would be a good time to ask for other duties, ones that don't require attentive listening skills until you are back to 100%.
- Inattentiveness or daydreaming.
- Fatigue. You can't concentrate when you're averaging four hours of sleep per night. Eight is the goal people.
- Formulating a reply. Especially the perfect comeback.
- Hunger. A friend recently told me he couldn't concentrate at a meeting; he was worried his stomach would growl. (It did, I heard it!)
- Headaches or other ailments. I speak from personal experience: headaches make it hard to focus, much less listen.
- Stress. A few well-spent minutes can reduce stress: Watch a funny YouTube video, call a friend, take a walk, dance, breathe, strike a favorite yoga pose (Happy Baby comes to mind).
- Critically evaluating the speaker. I used to work with a wonderful man who was the CEO of a large corporation. He routinely mispronounced words or used ones he out-and-out made up. One of my favorites was "flustrated." I'd get preoccupied with the word and stop listening.
- The rebuttal tendency. You're listening; you really are. And then the speaker makes an innocent mistake and you spend the entire rest of their talk wanting to say, "No! It wasn't Dustin Hoffman in that movie, it was Al Pacino!"

Trigger Words

When a customer uses words that trigger your defenses, it's normal to stop listening. We're human. Trigger words are any that evoke negative emotion. Some trigger words or phrases are almost universal, like the one I mentioned in a previous chapter: "It's our policy." Here are some others:

- You constantly, never, always . . .
- Make no mistake about it
- To be perfectly honest

- With all due respect
- Whatever
- Correct me if I'm wrong
- Don't get mad/upset but . . .
- I don't want to hurt your feelings
- Don't take this personally . . .
- Calm down

Now let's look at why some customers stop listening to you.

© Randy Glasbergen / glasbergen.com

**"No, Bob isn't hearing impaired.
Bob is listening impaired."**

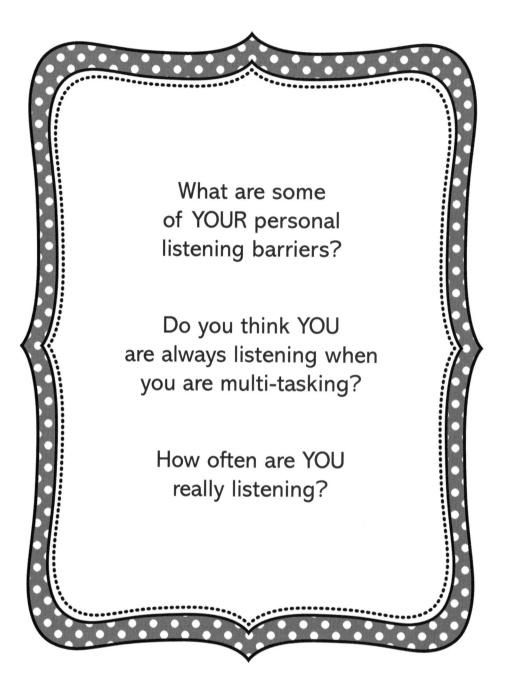

What are some
of YOUR personal
listening barriers?

Do you think YOU
are always listening when
you are multi-tasking?

How often are YOU
really listening?

Chapter 18

Listening:
How to Talk So Your
Customers Will Hear You

In the last chapter, we discussed the things that can hinder your listening process. But what about the reverse? Are there barriers you can knock down so that your customers are better able, and more willing, to hear you out? Yes, happily. And here they are:

Don't Use Jargon

"Okay, I got campers on 13 and a deuce at the door. Tell the cook I got 5 specials all day, and I need one of 'em killed. There's hot sh*t in the window, and I'm in the weeds. We've done 100 covers already tonight, and we still have 200 rollups to do. Let's turn 'em and burn 'em folks. I'm on a double and the couple on 12 is about to get 86'd!"

Jargon is the specialized language of a trade, profession, or similar group—especially when that language is barely understandable by outsiders. Jargon is fun to use with coworkers who speak the same language, as in the restaurant banter above. It's a way to feel bonded, special, united. But don't let yourself slip into jargon with your customers. They won't understand it, and they'll end up feeling frustrated, intimidated, lost, even angry. And here's another negative result of using jargon. Studies show that *"abstract language leads listeners to believe a speaker is lying more often than concrete language does."*

Research also shows that if you use jargon or technical talk with an uneducated person they are usually too intimidated to ask what you mean. If you use it with a highly educated person, they might be too prideful to ask what you mean. Either way, using jargon inhibits the dissemination of accurate information. It slows and warps the communication process.

Forbes has a "Jargon Madness" contest to find the most annoying terms currently in use. Here's what one writer said: *"The next time you feel the need to reach out, shift a paradigm, leverage a best practice, or join a tiger team, by all means do it. Just don't say you're doing it, because all that meaningless business jargon makes you sound like a complete moron."*

Hear, Hear

In the healthcare industry, the term SOB has a whole different meaning from the one you and I know. Once, at a training, the attendees began discussing SOB and I merrily chimed in that everyone knows one! "Shortness of breath?" they said. "Oh. Um, no," I said. "I thought you meant . . . "

Another great story I heard was from a hospital CEO who told me of an irate family who stormed into his office demanding to speak to him. "Your nurses just admitted that Robert has been on the floor for hours and now they are ready to move him." They had overheard the staff talking among themselves at the nurse's station. "How can you possibly leave a patient on the floor for hours and call yourselves caring professionals!?" they exclaimed. In hospital jargon, you see, floor means unit or department, not the linoleum. When that was explained, the family and the staff were both relieved.

Jargon can be catchy and easy to acquire. One of the most egregious examples is used in some RCFEs (Residential Care Facility for the Elderly) by unscrupulous staff. When a person has a terminal illness and is hovering between life and death, the term "circling the drain" can be heard. If the phrase is repeated often enough, even the best staff members will hear it slip from their mouths. They are horrified to hear themselves say it, but say it they do! Hang around someone who uses the F-word long enough and before long it will be a part of your speech, too. My sister routinely comes back from a week in the deep south with a Southern drawl as authentic as Scarlett O'Hara's. Patterns of speech are contagious.

Get To The Point

"Okay, ma'am. So there's a 404 error in your motherboard and I increased the bandwidth and added some RAM. That should jumpstart the biometrics, clean out your cloud, and patch in some pixels to stop the phishing. We found a napster in your quadcore, so we've put a ripper in your router and a shockwave in your serial port. You're lucky, 'cuz it coulda been malware in your adware and we'dve had to put more cache in your crawler. Anyways, we're all set and here's the bill."

I once had a website designer who talked to me for ten minutes and when he was finished, the only words I really understood were the short ones: *and*, *but*, *the*, *before* and *now*. As a technician (or physician, or plumber, or gas man), please ask how much detail the customer would like. They'll be glad to tell you. Some customers want the whole nine yards, all the detail. Some just want the facts: when, where, and how much? When you offer too much information without asking first, what is fascinating to you can be boring to them, and that's a barrier for sure. Getting to the point can also vary by gender. Women tend to bond by chitchat. We share more, yes, but we take a more circuitous route to the point than men do.

Any Questions?

- The information might be heard, but incorrectly. Be sure you have spoken clearly, and that your listener has heard you correctly, accurately.

- Maybe your customer listened well, but is still in the dark. My friend's son Mark came to her in misery. He had braces put on earlier in the week and he was in agony. When she pulled his lip out and looked inside, she saw that his cheeks were a swollen and bloody mess. She asked why he hadn't put the wax the dentist had given him on the sore spots. He said he did, but it wouldn't stick to his cheek. The dentist assumed Mark knew to place it on the metal braces in the spots that were causing the abrasions. Mark was putting the wax where it actually hurt.

Write It Down

Just because you can remember ten things doesn't mean your customer can. How about giving them a bulleted list of items they need to know, or steps they need to take. My brother had his wisdom teeth pulled and the assistant told him what he needed to do in the following days—right after he woke up from sedation. Needless to say he didn't remember a thing.

Right Words, Right Time

In medical settings especially, well-trained staff members know that when they can see a patient isn't listening, it's time to stop talking. When a frightening diagnosis or prognosis is heard for the first time, some people (patients and loved ones alike) can go straight into an emotional outburst. The reason is most often due to fear of the unknown and lack of control. Fear is a huge barrier and not only leads to not listening, but also to becoming defensive, argumentative, even angry. This is not a time to share important information. When the time is right, when the person is ready to listen, make the situation as conducive to listening as possible: Often there are "quiet rooms" in hospitals to accommodate this kind of conversation.

The right words need the right time, the right place, and also the right body language: look at the person, lean toward them, reduce the distance between you and the person talking. And when the conversation becomes two-way, don't bluff and nod when you don't understand. Ask for clarification.

Avoid the Overuse of Filler Words

You know what these are: "*um, okay, like,* and *you know*" are common filler words. Using these fillers excessively distracts the receiver's attention away from your message, casting doubt as to whether you really know what you're talking about. Suddenly, you are no longer credible. I find this habit so distracting, and let's be honest, so boring, that I start counting them. I'm a little fascinated by people who can't seem to speak their first language without using 160 "ums" during a single dinner conversation. And this was a famous attorney! That is not how you want to be remembered.

Noisy Work Space

You are used to it; they are not. Enough said.

What are the
more common barriers
to listening
in YOUR workplace?

What are some
of the common terms
YOU use that would be
considered jargon?

Chapter 19

Nonverbal Communication

How many languages do you know? Well, here's one you might forget to list: Kinesics, the language of non-verbal communication.

For example, your three year old bops his little sister on the head. You demand he apologize. "SORRY!" he bellows. You aren't happy, yet he did what you asked him to do. The problem is he didn't mean it. How do you know? Because you understand the language of nonverbal communication. His words said one thing; the tone and volume of his voice, and his reddened, tear-stained face, said another.

While we can almost always see the obvious contradiction between the words we hear and the body language we see in someone else, we are mostly oblivious to our own. Here's what I mean:

Tom is a flight nurse who worked with my sister, and I thought he'd be a good guest speaker for one of my classes. He agreed to do it, but admitted he was nervous. "Not to worry," I cooed. "You know your stuff." Tom held a retractable pen in his hand while he spoke and clicked it non-stop for the entire 90-minute talk. If you Google this behavior, you'll find it's associated with boredom, inattentive thinking, hiding something, and, oh, yeah, nervousness. I was so distracted by it, I didn't hear a word he said. I began by imagining various ways to grab it without interrupting his flow. By the time he was wrapping up, I had graduated to imagining how to stick it into his jugular. It was *that* disruptive.

Later, when my pulse had returned to normal, I mentioned the pen ever so casually and he was surprised. He had no recollection at all of even holding a pen, let alone that he spent the entire talk incessantly clicking it. He was utterly oblivious to his own non-verbal language. I've been admonished a time or two for my own unconscious body language. And I *teach* this stuff.

We are always communicating; sometimes verbally, always non-verbally. Without saying a single word, we communicate what we are thinking and feeling with our eyes, our hands, our posture, and the gestures we use—with either positive or negative results.

Joe Navarro is a nonverbal communications expert, executive coach and author of *Louder Than Words: Take Your Career From Average to Exceptional With the Hidden Power of Nonverbal Intelligence*. His definition of nonverbal is: *"…anything that communicates a thought, an idea, a mood, an intention, or a message but is not a word."* He points out that manners—smiling, holding a door, or letting someone else go first—are all examples of nonverbal behavior that reflect a person's character. He also lists color, clothing, even the cars people drive as examples of nonverbal communication.

"We know from studies that when we do things considered 'pro-social,' we are persuaded by it, we are seduced by it, we are influenced by it. So if I walk into a bank, and I have to walk all the way to where the manager is, I will feel differently about that bank than if I walk in and the manager gets up from behind his desk and walks toward me," Navarro says.

How about this? In 2012 Cathay Pacific flight attendants were in salary negotiations, but they didn't threaten an all-out strike. Instead, they threatened to fulfill only their most basic duties, which is to take care of safety measures and to get the passengers from one point to another. Period. One of the things they refused to provide was service with a smile. They'd serve, but they wouldn't smile. They knew how important smiling is; they knew not smiling would worry management, and it did.

Our nonverbal communication speaks volumes (no pun intended); it's more evident and more powerful than words. UCLA's Dr. Albert Mehrabian uses this model to illustrate how communication percentages break down.

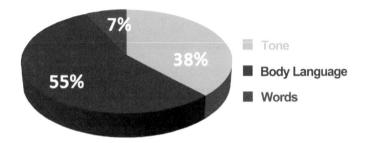

■ 7% of message pertaining to feelings and attitudes is in the words that are spoken.

■ 38% of message pertaining to feelings and attitudes is paralinguistic (the way that the words are said).

■ 55% of message pertaining to feelings and attitudes is in facial expression.

And here's yet another story about the danger of making assumptions. Thank you for taking me so seriously that you ran out and bought a book on body language. But beware. The "expert" author will tell you that a wink means this, and crossed arms mean that. They'll say leaning forward indicates interest; leaning away means indifference. Please make sure you keep your observations in context. Don't assume a universal truth about the way we speak with our bodies. Here's why:

I once had a meeting with a psychologist with whom I was collaborating on a project. We met on a hot summer day, and I was wearing a sleeveless summer dress—a bad choice in the land of extreme air conditioning. He was wearing a tweed jacket against the icy chill. I shivered as I took my seat in his office. During our chat, I kept shifting in my seat, trying to get warm. Suddenly he stopped mid-sentence and eyed me seriously. "Are you attracted to me?" he asked.

Um . . . excuse me . . . what? He said my body language—leaning forward and rubbing my arms—suggested that I was. Good grief. I wasn't flirting; I was trying to stave off frostbite! Now I was terrified that if I licked my dry lips he would jump over the desk. Talk about putting a rock wall in the way of our *professional* relationship. So be careful about being a body language expert. The wink that handsome man at the bar gave you might simply be a nervous tic.

Some gestures, however, do have meanings you can trust. That tried-and-true symbol of universal disgust showcasing one's middle finger is a pretty sure sign you've pissed someone off. Generally speaking, though, don't assume.

"Your body language would suggest you're
not having the best time on our first date."

Two final thoughts:

* ***Body language is informed by culture.*** Important global leaders, including U.S. presidents, have committed some publicly embarrassing social gaffes when using gestures that mean one thing in our culture; quite another in other cultures. Remember the thrashing

basketball star LeBron James took from the British press when he dared to sling a friendly arm around the Duchess of Cambridge? Prince William and Kate were attending a game and posed for the famous photo with James. The headlines, "LeBron James Causes Royal Stir," left the entire UK in an uproar. James had unwittingly broken one of the most rigid rules of royal etiquette: Never touch a royal. A royal etiquette expert (yes, there really is a guy out there making his living being one) was quoted as saying, "Americans are much more tactile than we Brits and this is another example of an American being too touchy feely with British royalty. You'd have thought they'd have learned by now."

Our thumb-and-forefinger "okay" sign, the '60's peace sign (also used as the victory sign during World War II), even the ubiquitous thumbs-up are all seen as offensive gestures by one culture or another. Did you know that crossing an ankle over your knee and displaying the sole of your shoe is a major offense in Middle Eastern cultures. What about greetings? Do you kiss on one cheek or both cheeks; do you bow or shake hands? It all depends on what part of the globe you inhabit.

If you conduct business exclusively in the U.S., then learning the subtleties of American body language will suffice. But if you have an international clientele, it will be worth your while to study things like insulting gestures, eye contact, personal space, and touch frequency.

- *Make sure your nonverbal message supports your verbal message.* The young man in the video store who told me to "have a nice day" in an earlier chapter is a perfect example. His words said one thing, his body language another. Think about the ways you can say "I'm sorry." Assertively (eye contact, sincere tone), aggressively (finger point, loud voice), passive-aggressively (eye roll), and passively (eyes downcast, soft voice). Same words; four different meanings. How you say it can completely change or even nullify, the apology.

People want to do business with those who make them feel comfortable. Sincerity and good manners are key.

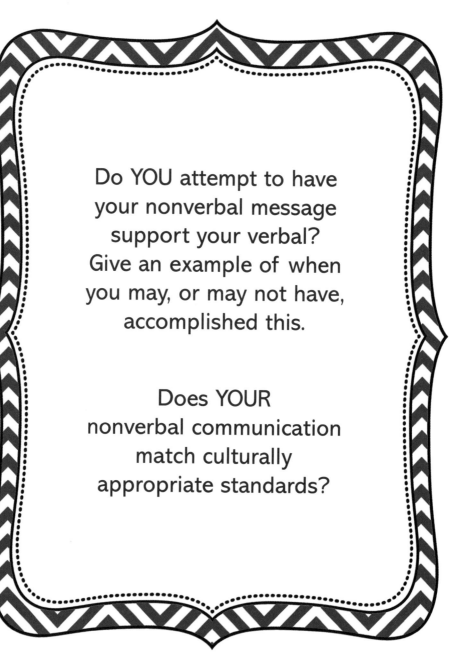

Do YOU attempt to have
your nonverbal message
support your verbal?
Give an example of when
you may, or may not have,
accomplished this.

Does YOUR
nonverbal communication
match culturally
appropriate standards?

Chapter 20

Body Language:
Giving New Meaning to
"Actions Speak Louder Than Words"

Deafness has left me acutely aware of both
the duplicity that language is capable of and
the many expressions the body cannot hide.
~ Terry Galloway

What you do speaks so loud
that I cannot hear what you say.
~ Ralph Waldo Emerson

I was playing blackjack at a fundraiser once, and was doing so well the dealer asked me if I'd ever played at a casino. "Not yet," I crowed, "but I think I need to start." "Don't," he warned. "Wait, what?" But I was cleaning up that night! To which he said I was the most obvious player he had ever seen. I don't have much of a poker face apparently. I guess it was my irrepressible grin, squeal of delight, and barely concealed bounce whenever I got a great hand that gave me away. I've always worn my heart on my sleeve. Damn it.

And truth be told, I know it. Been busted more than a few times for it. Once it was even captured on videotape so even the princess of protest (that would be me) could see it clear as day. There I was at my brother's wedding sizing up another guest's outfit with what I *thought* was a bland expression, carefully concealing my real feelings. But the camera caught the truth, and it was not a pretty picture. I didn't approve of this woman's choice in wedding attendee attire and you could see my opinion written like a headline in my body language. I was leaning back slightly, arms crossed, with an unforgiving frown on my face, my eyes wide as I surveyed the woman's ensemble top to bottom. Not my finest moment.

People are watching. So we need to pay close attention to what our nonverbal body language is broadcasting so clearly. We're pretty good at reading what others' bodies are telling us. But (as I have so boldly confessed), we aren't so hot at monitoring our own.

I watch my doctor's face like a hawk, looking for any sign of impending doom in the future of my health. I scrutinize the expressions on my CPA's face, too, for cues that might foretell my financial condition. There is so much written on the human face.

A study from Ohio State University revealed a list of 21 different emotions to be seen on the human face. It used to be just six: happiness, sadness, surprise, fear, disgust and anger; now there are 15 more.

Here are just a few of the gazillion variations we can observe in the human face:

- **Eyes**: are they wide, staring, cast down, steadily gazing, looking away, unblinking, damp, closed, closed tightly, darting glances?
- **Eye brows**: are they furrowed, raised up, down low, blinking fast, or very slow?
- **Mouth**: is the lower lip trembling, is the upper lip stiff, is it pouting, kissing, pinched, open in an "o" shape, tongue stuck out, tongue tip reaching for upper lip, or biting the lower lip?

- **Hair**: are you twirling it, brushing it off your face, running your hands through it?

And then there's head movement (bobbing, shaking "no", tilted in disbelief); chin movements; face rubbing; bridge of nose pinching—each tiny nuance conveys volumes, right?

There's no way to control our propensity to blush crimson when nervous or embarrassed. Or blanch white (or turn grey) under pressure or grief. Not much we can do to stop the sweat from beading up on our foreheads

BOTTOMS UP   bert silva

"IF YOU'RE GOING TO MAKE FRIENDS, LARRY... YOU MUST LEARN THERE IS A FINE LINE BETWEEN EYE CONTACT AND THE PIERCING STARE OF A PSYCOPATH."

if that's the way we process a bad case of stage fright. I was speaking at an event with a man who is not a speaker. Tom had bullets of sweat forming at his hairline. I felt sorry for him but was oddly fascinated at the same time. I told him, "Hey, no one ever died from public speaking, okay?" But he was inconsolable, and I thought that Tom just might be the first!

So there are some things we are helpless to control; but if we can be more aware of them, we can learn techniques that will change our body's knee-jerk responses to things. How we react to life's hard situations psychologically can change how our bodies react, too. Even blushing, blanching, and sweating!

Now let's add sound to the picture. Our voices (regardless of the words we are uttering) contain tone, inflection, pitch, rate and volume. Adopting a neutral tone might be safest approach, but research shows that 65% of customers prefer a "casual" tone. Yet more studies conclude that customers are likely to interpret a casual tone in a delicate situation as being insensitive or condescending. A monotone or flat voice is telling the customer "I am so bored!" A high pitch conveys enthusiasm, or distress. A rapid pace with the volume turned up indicates disapproval, unhappiness, irritation. How on earth do we learn to identify all these variables in order to put our, uh, best face forward?

Let Louis C.K. show you how! A laugh-out-loud scene on his TV show "Louie" finds Matthew Broderick desperately trying to get the right delivery out of Louie in the role of a cop. In the movie, Louie's character must tell a young man (Broderick) not to enter a crime scene because his father has been killed. Watch it by looking for "Ep 106 CopMovie" on YouTube. It's a fine (and hilarious) lesson in body language.

So at the risk of driving you into seclusion forever, I have three more elements for you to consider in the infinite world of body language: Proxemics (or personal space), Touch, and Annoying Habits.

Proxemics: Remember *Seinfeld's* recurring character, the "close talker," who got uncomfortably close to everyone? Those who work in the medical field are famous for that, forgetting that not everyone knows what's coming. How hard would it be to tell you they have to take your blood pressure *before* they reach out and grab your arm? Every culture, every individual has a unique comfort zone around personal space. Respecting it is paramount in the reach for great customer service.

Touch: We've all read about the basic human need for another's touch. Did you know that touching someone on the arm, hand, or shoulder for as little as 1/40 of a second creates a human bond? That touch is also used as a way to communicate status and power? (Think about that one for a minute.) That women tend to use touch to convey care, concern and nurturing; while men are more likely to use touch to assert power and control?

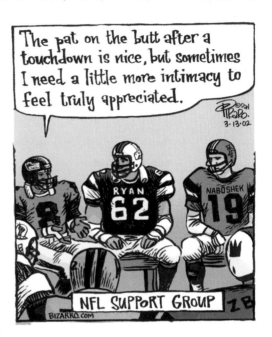

I'm a hugger; many of you are not. I know this, and yet I continue to find myself in the middle of a full-on body hug before your stiff-as-a-board body reminds me: oh yeah, not everyone likes this. You'd think I'd learn.

Annoying Habits: These are the myriad little habits we have that are so often completely unconscious: Clicking a ballpoint pen (remember Tom?), jingling the change in your pocket, drumming your fingers, tapping your pencil, laughing too loudly, clipping your nails, flossing your teeth (please, not even in front of your best friend!). Tossing your hair back, bouncing your knees, arching your back to get rid of a kink, picking at the mole on your neck. You *say* a lot when you engage in these habits. Curb them!

Wow. That's a lot to take in. But don't join that monastery just yet. Start by asking for feedback. Make a video of yourself in conversation . . . and watch it. You'll learn something. I *know* I'm not the only one who has ever been busted.

How do YOU
respond to someone's
body language?
Do you attempt to
mirror it or ignore it?

Have you ever had
someone critique YOUR
body language?
Your employees?

Chapter 21

Smile

Yep, there is an entire science around smiling. People have been conducting serious studies for years. Here's one done at a college campus library:

The researchers wanted to find out how friendliness related to competence. They instructed one of the librarians to show no positive affect while checking out books. Students would walk up to her and she would take their library cards and scan their books, offering no eye contact, no smile. A second librarian was asked to do three things: make eye contact, smile, and use the patron's name (which could easily be seen on their library card). She didn't have to stop or even slow down to do these three things; it took no more time to show positive affect than it did to show no affect at all. When the students left, the surveyors were outside, asking not how friendly they were, but how *competent* they were. The findings revealed that more students thought the nicer one was better at her job. The second librarian was not better, not faster than the first. But she was nicer. And that, apparently, translates to competence. My nurse friend said the same thing happens in her profession. She told me the nurses with weakest clinical skills were the ones getting letters saying "Best nurse ever." Because they were the ones hanging out and chatting with the patients.

"A man without a smiling face must not open a shop." ~ Chinese Proverb

Pretty much says it all, doesn't it? Smiling is the first and most obvious step to great customer service and it doesn't cost a thing. Smiling, as simple and unassuming as it seems, is one of the most important interactions you can have with your customers. Smiling is a universal gesture, breaking through all barriers—age, gender, race, religion, you name it. It's the start, and often the end, of in any conversation.

In study after study, the unsurprising conclusion is that customer satisfaction increases greatly when an authentic smile is given. That seemingly small gift makes us feel valued, which is a good argument for in-person sales and services (versus online).

The wellness person in me wants to tell you:

- We are drawn to people who smile; it's an element of attraction.
- Smiling changes our mood. It releases endorphins and makes us feel happier. It works better than chocolate, they say.
- Smiling is contagious; good to know when you have a grumpy customer.
- Smiling relieves stress.
- Smiling makes you healthier.

Leo Widrich wrote a great article on the science of smiling. *"Whenever we smile, there are 2 potential muscles we activate. The first one is the zygomaticus major and it controls the corners of your mouth. Whenever this muscle only is activated, it's not actually a genuine smile. Scientists call this also the 'social' smile. The second muscle, known to show sincerity is the obicularis occuli and it encircles our eye socket. The true smile is also called the duchenne smile, named after the famous scientist who first separated the 'mouth corners'-only smile, from the 'eye socket' one."*

We intuitively know this, and most of us can tell a sincere smile from fake one a mile away. We know (and love) the people we know are smiling even when *all* we can see are their eyes.

Faking It

Another smiling study was published in the journal *Personnel Psychology*. They looked at employees who were faking their smiles to see if doing that on a daily basis could exact an emotional and physical toll.

"[Employees] could smile because they genuinely like their customers or they are simply happy, and in that case they are not engaging in what we call 'emotional labor' because they are not faking," explained lead researcher David Wagner, Ph.D. of Singapore Management University, in an email to the *Huffington Post*. *"When they put on that happy face but don't really feel it—that's when we start to have problems."*

Once employers acknowledge the toll that emotional work takes, they can help their employees cope by making simple changes. For example, they could provide "offstage" areas where workers can relax and drop the mask; or offer workshops on pleasant behavior as a strategy that benefits them *and* the company. Or why not simply hire people who don't find it so difficult to smile in the first place?

I was hired to speak to a group of doctors about customer service. It was a mandatory meeting, held on an evening when two super sports teams were in playoffs for the championship. Hey, thanks scheduler. I had a tough audience.

But we ended up having a good time and laughed a lot. At the end of the evening I asked each doctor what one thing they would do differently. One of them said, "Smile." I looked at him, waiting for the punchline. But no, he was serious.

When I think back on it, it was actually one of the best things he could start doing.

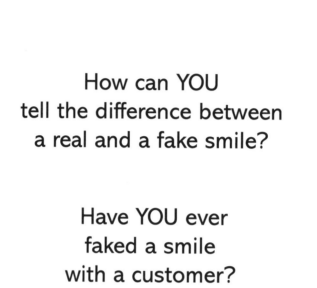

How can YOU
tell the difference between
a real and a fake smile?

Have YOU ever
faked a smile
with a customer?
With an employee?
If so, how did it effect
the interaction?

Chapter 22

Yes, it is . . . All About Attitude

You know that waitress who seems to forget a lot but she's so much fun and so pleasant that you tip her really well anyway? Or the man at the post office you will wait in a longer line for because he always makes you smile? We like positive people. I am not suggesting you can just be nice and who cares if you're good at your job. I *am* saying, "Be positive."

"Hire for attitude, train for skills" or "Character counts for more than credentials." Have you heard those adages? I find it interesting that many businesses don't want to hire people who are industry veterans. They know that long-established habits and deeply ingrained attitudes can come with all those years, and many of them are negative.

When I hire people I do want certain skills, but what I have found over the years is that behavior, character, and attitude are more important. I can train for the skills I need. I can't train for authenticity. I can teach you how to fill out my preparation checklist for speaking engagements; I can't teach you to have a positive attitude. That one is a choice. So I use "behavioral based hiring" when I'm looking for new staff. I look for people who see the world through a sparkling glass (preferably a champagne flute!) that's always half full (not half empty). I look for the upbeat way you see the world, the way you view the environment around you, the optimism you have about your future and yes, the respectful way you treat my clients.

I want you to meet Claudette. She was our secretary when I worked in a large office for a school district. Experience had taught us that we could learn from Claudette's perspective, so whenever a prospective new-hire came in to interview, we'd make them sit with Claudette for 10 minutes before we began our panel interview. The prospect didn't know it, but that few minutes with our secretary was the real start of the interview. Claudette would chat with them informally, paying attention to what they said and how they behaved in a setting much less tense than the four-person panel of future bosses would be. With Claudette, the applicants did not feel compelled to be on their best behavior and we learned a lot.

If we had a candidate we really liked, we'd come out of the interview with our fingers crossed, hoping Claudette would not give us the thumbs down. "So what do you think? Did you like him (her)?" we'd ask. Mostly her assessments were short, to the point, and coincided with our general impressions. Occasionally though, she would shake her head, "Uh uh. She spent way too much time glancing at herself in the mirror behind me. Pretty conceited." Or "Nope. He's a bigot and he doesn't even know it." Or "Not really. He was rude, and condescending." Here's what prompted that last pronouncement: In response to one of her casual questions, one candidate said to her, "Let me put this in terms you can understand." Ouch.

This one is for any hiring managers out there:

We were hiring for an assistant and I happened to stay late in the office the evening prior to get some work done before a full-day of interviewing. The main phone to the office rang and I answered it. Normally our secretary would have picked it up. A woman on the phone was asking for the fastest way to get to our office. I asked her what time she was coming because traffic varies, and she told me 2 p.m. the next day. I gave her directions, then asked, "Do you have an interview with us?" Her response? "Is that any of your business?" Wow. Actually it was very much my business.

After her interview the next day, she said, "It was nice meeting you." To which

I replied, "We already kind of met. We spoke on the phone last night when you called to ask for directions." She blanched. Her résumé was excellent, she interviewed well, but her rudeness on the phone was inexcusable. She didn't even offer an excuse; she knew she'd blown it. So this tip is from my business mentor and dear friend Ed Cox, *"The way it begins is the way it goes."* If they are showing you a bad attitude before you even hire them, don't.

I like that attitude is a choice. That puts the power in my hands. I won't allow you to ruin my day when you cut me off the freeway or give me the stink eye, because before I even get out of bed, I *choose* to have a good day. I also choose to make *your* day wonderful, too. Imagine how many more satisfied customers there would be if every business had a staff who decided, even for just one day, to make others' happiness a priority.

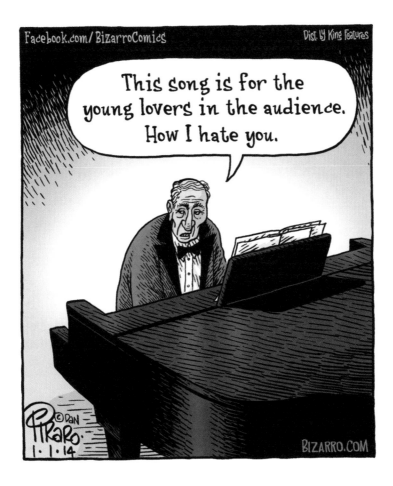

Keith Harrell, a business expert, claims, *"Dealing with negative attitudes in the workplace is one of the biggest challenges facing businesses, managers and employees."* And let me add customers. I didn't come into your business for the crappy attitude you are giving me.

Ways to improve your attitude:

- Hang out with positive people
- Practice positive-self talk and affirmations. I always ask the crowd when I speak, "How many of you woke up this morning, looked in the mirror and said, 'Damn, I am looking good'"? It should be all of us!
- Accentuate the positive. Make a list. You have a job, your health, great friends . . . you add on from there. I volunteer at a great local place where people who are out of work get training and help finding a job. One of the classes I teach is on, yep, attitude. Every time I go there I am reminded how lucky I am to have a job, and that it's one I love.
- Don't give power to toxic, negative people.
- Proven attitude adjustments:
  - Find quiet time
  - Find something to look forward to
  - Commit conscious acts of kindness
  - Enjoy nature
  - Be creative

"I am convinced that life is 10% what happens to me, and 90% how I react to it." ~ *Charles Swindoll*

It really is up to you.

Does YOUR company,
"Hire for attitude,
and train for skills?"
What is the benefit
in doing so?

What are some ways
you improve YOUR attitude
if you wake up on the
wrong side of the bed?

Chapter 23

Assumptions

Assume, and you make an ass
out of you and me.
~ Unknown

My friend Christine got a job at a high-end jewelry store (think Tiffany's or Rodeo Drive). On the first day she was permitted to serve customers on her own (post-training), Christine was excited. When her co-workers suggested she take the new customer who had just walked in, "for experience," she was naïve and eager. Her co-workers, not so much. The new customer was wearing old jeans, a t-shirt, and three days' growth of grey beard stubble. The sales staff watched with interest (you can imagine what they had assumed). Inside of one hour, Christine's first customer spent more than $300,000. Everyone in the shop learned a valuable lesson that day about assumptions. As Julia Roberts' character in *Pretty Woman* said to the shopkeeper who assumed she couldn't possibly buy anything: *"Big Mistake."*

And here's another just for good measure: My brother-in-law, Rick, lived on a rural acreage in Washington State. One day, his 4-year-old son, Alec, was kicked by a mule and Rick rushed him to the emergency room of the nearest hospital.

Whereupon the intake nurse took one look at Rick (who had been working on a broken pipe and was muddy head-to-toe) and asked whether he had insurance. Fair enough. Until she added, "Do you have . . . (long pause) a job?" Rick sighed, saying "Yes, I work in environmental services." "Oh," the nurse asked, "like a garbage man?" Rick steadied himself. "No, like a chemical engineer for the Environmental Protection Agency." Alec was fine as it turns out. The mule had done no real damage. But it took a while for Rick's blood pressure to drop back to normal . . . and for the nurse's crimson shade of shame to fade.

Allow me to quote from my first book:

> "We make assumptions about everything. It's part of the human condition; we can't live without them. The trick is to determine which assumptions are useful and which ones are harmful. Assumptions about other people, based on looks, color, or even body art can be harmful to everyone, including the assumer.

> "One of the major discussions we have in my **Using Good Judgment** course is all about assumptions. Simply defined, an assumption is a belief that something is true without proof or demonstration. We make assumptions based on data culled from our life experiences. We couldn't live our lives without making them. Assumptions help us gather information to make sense of the world around us. For example, I assume that other drivers run red lights, so I never head out across the intersection the second my light turns green. In that case, assuming could save my life."

So how does making assumptions affect the world of customer service? Read 'em and weep:

Businesses . . .

- assume their customers are loyal and will never leave them.
- assume their customers are faithful to the company name, when it might be to the one employee we really love. An international bank bought out the hometown bank where I have my accounts. I stayed with it during the transition because of the strong relationship I had with one of the bankers. Well, Big International Bank let her go after 25 years of service. When she left, so did her customers. We followed *her*, not the name of the bank.
- assume that being the only game in town makes them impervious to failure. If you have read this book in order (it's okay if you didn't 'cuz I'm going to say it again), you'll remember that people *will* drive farther and pay more for better customer service.
- assume customers will tolerate complexity. (If I can't figure it out in a few minutes, I'm outta there. Aren't you?)
- assume customers care if you're having a bad day. I was in a large box store once and there was a young man behind the counter in their food court. He was unforgivably rude to the elderly gentleman in front of me. When it was my turn, I asked him what on earth caused him to be so mean. "I don't even want to be here," he grum-

bled. "Someone called in sick and my shift is over but my boss made me stay to cover for him." Well guess what? I don't care. I told him if his manager had heard what I just heard, she'd let the poor guy go home. Permanently.

- assume you know what your customers want. If you communicate well on a regular basis, you *should* be able to anticipate what people want. But even years of history is not enough to support the assumption that just because Joe Schmo wanted his steak rare for the last decade, he wants it that way today. The one time you bring him that rare steak without asking is the one time he'll say he wanted it medium. And there goes your regular customer, down the street, where they *do* ask.
- assume that a few bad experiences and the occasional unhappy customer won't hurt you. Need I remind you of this equation? Angry customer + Internet = very big megaphone!?
- assume most customers complain when there is a problem. Most unhappy people tell other people. Only 25% will ever tell you.
- assume fewer complaints mean people are happy. Did you know that in-person complaint rates are actually declining? The majority feel that saying something won't do any good. What does *that* say about customer service today?

It's worth repeating: Assumptions are a normal part of the human experience. Think about all the assumptions we make about individuals based on age, gender, race, attire, accent, physical abilities, personal style, education, even the cars we drive? Then ask yourself whether assumptions hinder your ability to give great customer service.

What assumptions
do YOU make
about your customers?
About your employees?

What assumptions are
YOUR employees making?
About their customers,
and about each other?

What steps can YOU take
to stop or limit them?

Chapter 24

Customer Complaints

"*Y*our most unhappy customers are your greatest source of learning." So said Bill Gates, and he's doing okay, so we would do well to listen. If you get nauseous, desert mouth, and damp under the arms every time a customer asks to see the manager, you probably shouldn't be in customer service.

If you're a natural-born manager, then take Gates' wisdom to heart. And make it even sweeter by looking at a customer complaint as an opportunity to make a change. You might just win this one over for life. Listening and then actively

"So, as you can see, customer satisfaction is up considerably since phasing out the complaint forms."

trying to resolve the problem gives you insight, reduces stress (for you *and* for your customer), and ends by ratcheting up your sense of competence. That's a lot of wins out of what could have been a lose-lose situation.

If you're a numbers person, here's more to think about:

- 82% of consumers say the number one factor that leads to a great customer service experience is a quick resolution.
- A 2% increase in customer retention has the same effect as decreasing costs by 10%.
- Customers are increasingly frustrated with the level of service they experience: 91% because they have to contact a company multiple times for the same reason; 90% because they're put on hold for a long time; and 89% because they have to repeat their issue to multiple representatives.
- 70% of customers will do business with you again if you resolve their complaints.
- For every customer complaint there are 26 other unhappy customers who have remained silent.
- 96% of unhappy customers don't complain, however 91% of those will simply leave and never come back.

I wonder why the front desk clerk so often fails to ask me how my stay was at checkout time. It's not like there's a big line or any pressing reason to hurry. Maybe they just don't want to hear anything negative. Not very smart. Hearing about a guest's experience at your hotel is a way to learn and improve. Besides, wouldn't you much rather hear it from me than read about it online? Remember, satisfied customers tell four to six people about their experience. And when writing a review on-line, that number multiplies dramatically.

Yes the coffee *is* cold.

I recently called the headquarters of a national chain restaurant with a complaint about one of their managers. They listened—really listened—and sent me a gift certificate. Good so far. A few days later, their California division director called me and we talked about the issue again. He wanted to be sure I had been heard and was satisfied with the way they chose to handle it. The brand succeeded in winning me back (though I probably won't go back to the place of the original sin until that errant manager is erring somewhere else).

Handling feedback well takes practice. Up to 95% of customers will give you a second chance if you handle their complaint successfully *and* in a timely manner. Don't just agree that there is an issue; *do something*.

Greg Ciotti wrote a great article on *Help Scout* about handling complaints. Here are some of his suggestions:

1. Give Credence to Each Customer. Ciotti quotes Myers Barnes: *"Treat every customer as if they have 10,000 Twitter followers."*

2. Remember that Complaints Contain Insight. It is difficult to see your own foibles. As the hard-working manager, you might not see your sandwich maker using the same knife for everything. But your customers do.

3. Record and Organize Meaningful Complaints. Don't find out at an end-of-month team meeting that 18 of your staff got the same complaint. Develop a tracking system so you can discover the issue and do something about it.

4. Identify What Sort of Complainers They Are. An academic publication from University of Florida on customer complaints presents a strong case for categorizing complainers through a selection of customer archetypes.

- *The Meek Customer*: Generally averse to complaining, but warrants a mention because you may need to inquire more deeply to get them to reveal exactly what's wrong.

- *The Aggressive Customer*: Outspoken and not shy about letting you know what's on their mind. Your best bet is to avoid being aggressive back and instead react with "What else may I help you with?" Show that you're ready and willing to hear them out.

- *The High Roller*: Your "enterprise" customer; they likely pay you well and demand premium support for it. While no customers are fond of excuses, this customer really hates hearing them.

- *The Chronic Complainer*: This customer will contact you a lot, but that doesn't mean that their issues should be dismissed. Patience is required here, but once satisfied, this customer will have no qualms about singing your praises to others.

- *The Barnacle*: Although the publication identifies this type as the "rip-off" customer, I find the barnacle label to be more accurate. This customer is never happy and isn't really looking for a satisfactory response; they are just trying to get something they don't deserve. Everything is "not good enough," unless they're getting a handout. Your best bet is to maintain your composure and respond as objectively as possible.

5. *Don't be Passive Aggressive.* This "don't" is so important, we're giving it a section all its own in an upcoming chapter.

6. *If you have to transfer them, explain why.*

7. *Use supportive questioning.*

- Clarify the problem
- Use open-ended questions
- Probe reasons and evidence
- Define their viewpoint, perspective and assumptions

8. *Remember, time is of the essence.*

9. *Verify the resolution.*

Then do your happy dance. That wasn't Greg's point; it was mine.

And finally, remember that ***perception equals reality—for the perceiver***. You might not agree that your hostess played favorites with the seating, but if that's what the customer perceived, then that's what is real for him. And true or not, unless you resolve his complaint, he will trumpet his truth to the world.

How do YOU
view a complaint?

As a problem
or opportunity?

Chapter 25

Dealing with Difficult People

An argument is not the best way to start a workshop, but in the following case, it was a valuable discussion-starter. At a customer service training I was doing for a city, each department rep insisted *they* had the most difficult customers. I think parking enforcement won that fight (rightfully so), but the reality is we have all encountered difficult customers in the workplace. From the diner who claims the too-salty soup will raise his blood pressure, to the neighborhood watch captain who wants the crack dealers off his corner, difficult situations come up in every working life.

Whether they are internal from other departments or external, from actual customers—people can be challenging. Sometimes simply witnessing a disgruntled person in front of us in line (completely apart from the workplace), will engage us and prompt us to take sides. Think about which side you typically choose? I tend to choose the person who is calmest; calm in a non-passive aggressive way of course.

It's Not ALWayS A PLeaSure To Serve You, We JuSt Say THat!

So here are some tips:

- *Apologize.* When approaching a customer who has come to you with a complaint, you can apologize for others' mistakes but don't make excuses, justify their actions, or criticize another person or department. And offer a real apology; not "We're sorry you feel that way." Here's how Jeff Bezos handled a mistake his mega-company made.

  Jeffrey P. Bezos says:

  This is an apology for the way we previously handled illegally sold copies of 1984 and other novels on Kindle. Our "solution" to the problem was stupid, thoughtless, and painfully out of line with our principles. It is wholly self-inflicted, and we deserve the criticism we've received. We will use the scar tissue from this painful mistake to help make better decisions going forward, ones that match our mission.

  With deep apology to our customers,

  Jeff Bezos
  Founder & CEO
  http://Amazon.com

I took my mom to the ER and was told she needed an x-ray in order to diagnose the problem. We were told it would be about forty-five minutes. Two hours later we were still waiting. When I told the nurse how long it had been, she started to bad-mouth the x-ray department. "They always do this," she lamented, "I am so sick of them." Not okay. **Don't throw another department (or business, or individual) under the bus.**

A blameless apology is the way she should have handled it. "I'm sorry," would have been better. "Let me see what's going on." Handle it, and then bring the problem up with the managers of both departments at a later time.

- **Ask for help.** A man in one of my classes told me "no way" could he ever ask for help; he claimed it made him look weak.

Really? I think it shows we are human. Not everyone gets along. Sometimes there are personality clashes. If you are truly a committed team member, you'll feel comfortable asking someone else for help.

- **Look for the win/win.** Do away with the "us" versus "them" mentality. The ideal resolution is when both parties walk away happy.

- **Listen for the facts.** Getting the facts is paramount, but the facts are pretty impossible to hear when you're being yelled at.

"Taking abuse" is not part of anyone's job description. So there's never any reason to tolerate yelling. I stop hearing people when the yelling starts. My mind just shuts down because it feels so uncomfortable. So, without telling them to "calm down" (which actually produces the opposite response), use what I say instead: "It sounds like you have a valid point; can we discuss this?"

- ***Don't take it personally.*** It's not about you.

I have a sister who works as an RN in the emergency room. One harrowing night, a patient began screaming for the drugs she came in for (interestingly they wouldn't give morphine for a "bad back"), ending her tirade with "you b**ch!" To which my sister responded, "That's *Nurse* B**ch to you." The patient actually laughed. Situation handled. Don't let screaming customers hurt your feelings. Use positive self-talk. Remind yourself, as Stuart Smalley did on *Saturday Night Live*, "I'm good enough, I'm smart enough, and doggone it people like me."

- ***Personalize the interaction.***

Listen to the difference: 1. I ask for the manager and he comes to my table saying "Yes?" 2. I ask for the manager and he comes to my table with an outstretched hand saying "Hi, I'm the manager, John Smith. And you are? How can I help you today?" All of a sudden it's Jean and John, two people; not some angry customer and a nameless manager.

- ***Develop problem-solving guidelines and be flexible with them.***

Pacific Gas & Electric does something smart at the beginning of their meetings. They get all the important "what ifs" out of the way by asking this: "If there is a problem, who volunteers to call 911? Who will perform CPR?" They decide who is empowered to do what task so they can get down to business. Do you have a designated "go-to" person when your customers have a problem? Here's one example:

At a five-star restaurant in Southern California, there was one server (out of 50!) who was so diplomatic, so articulate, so gracious that she could calm the waters even when the table was on fire (which happened once when the dish being flamed at tableside caught the diner's gauzy dress on fire). She was the "go-to" server for patrons with a problem. Some people just have that gift. Find one.

Some guidelines:

- Listen. Let them finish.

- Understand the problem.
- Give a blameless apology.
- Find a resolution.
- Follow up.

There may come a time when it is appropriate to fire a customer. Chip Bell wrote in an article for *Entrepreneur* magazine,

"We all know customers are not always right—whether their behavior oversteps the bounds of civility or they issue invalid claims or unreasonable demands or make an out-and-out error.

But owing to their status as the lifeblood of any organization, customers are always worthy of fair and considerate treatment. Wise organizations focus on helping them 'discover' an error or misconception on their own rather than rubbing their noses in it.

There will come times, however, when it is appropriate to consider firing a customer. When the emotional or economic toll exacted from serving continually abusive or extremely high-maintenance, low-profit customers starts to outweigh the return on the investment, it is time to impose a customer exit strategy. Weigh the costs and then say goodbye."

How do YOU
typically deal with
an unpleasant customer?
How do your employees?

Give an example of how
you could use the tips in
this chapter to improve
upon your interactions with
an unhappy customer.

Chapter 26

When Customers Lose Control

Never underestimate the power of the irate customer. Customers get angry all the time and for a variety of reasons; sometimes justified, sometimes not. Occasionally it escalates from mildly annoyed to crazy-mad. And even when we know we are helpless to change their feelings, it's upsetting. Learn to handle this volatile state for two very good reasons: 1. The continued success of your company depends on it, and 2. The mental (even physical) health of your staff does, too.

First up? **Breathe.** Yep, it's that simple. Stress, anxiety and panic can all cause shallow breathing, which leads to more stress, anxiety, forgetfulness, and lack of concentration. It can even cause fainting. Now there's a real show-stopper.

Most of us don't think about our breathing, but next time you're under pressure, make the effort to notice your breathing. Deep, diaphragmatic breaths will bring needed oxygen to your whole being, ease your troubled mind, and calm your shaky body. Practice deep breathing while watching a scary movie or other contrived stressful setting, so when you are faced with a real-life fight-or-flight situation, you'll breathe deeply automatically.

Stay in control. When I was in graduate school, I took an "Interpersonal Conflict" class. Destructive conflict brings on a phenomenon called the "escalatory spiral," which our professor called the "conflict dance." Escalatory spirals have only one direction: upward and outward. Here's how it works:

When one person raises his voice, the other unconsciously raises hers as well. When person #1 escalates even further, person #2 rises to his level. Before you know it, both people are both yelling. Guess who loses in that situation? Pretty much everybody, including your company. So please. We're grownups; there is no reason to stoop to such phrases as "He started it!" Think, breathe, and maintain a level tone of voice.

When we respond to an angry customer . . .

- Acknowledge the other person's feelings. When people feel intensely, their feelings become facts. Don't minimize them.
- Clarify the specific issue involved (e.g., Are they mad because you make products they deem toxic to all life on the earth as their tirade suggests? Or because your accountant made an error on their order of oven cleaner?)
- Gauge the intensity and importance of the issue—to the customer! —not you.
- Invite the complainant to join *with* you to find a solution.
- Make an optimistic statement. You want to work this out.

I was flying home to California and the woman at the United Airlines Gate asked flyers with smaller bags to put an ID tag on them. As a courtesy, she began handing out tags to those in line. One passenger came utterly unglued. He began screaming at her. How dare she ask him to do that? Like she had just asked him to strip naked and say the alphabet backwards or something. He was out of control, over something absurdly petty (admittedly: petty—*to us*). As a mere observer, I was shocked and confused, and *my* heart was racing. What was *she* feeling? No one could tell, because she handled it beautifully. She didn't engage in the rage. She just looked at him and calmly called security, who dealt with him deftly and pulled him off the flight. Impressive, right?

Not everyone has the benefit of having security (oh, wouldn't *that* be nice? Watch Anjelah Johnson as Bon Qui Qui on YouTube, calling for "sa-coor-ity" every time a customer orders something complicated at King Burger). But every business should establish a protocol, a well-defined (and well-rehearsed) set of steps in place, to avoid catastrophe when customers go berserk.

Does YOUR company
have a protocol on how to
handle enraged customers?
If so, is it in writing?
Are all staff members aware
of this protocol?

Practice how YOU
would adjust your response
to an angry customer...
over the phone, via email,
or in person.

Chapter 27

Email Etiquette

Ah, email! It's a convenient, I-don't-really-want-to-talk-to-you, send-it-anytime, check-it-*all*-the-time, indispensable part of our business lives. And with the dozens, sometimes hundreds, of messages to read and manage, do you really need . . .

- A sappy chain email from the office manager of your car mechanic?
- A blue joke, complete with graphics, from a friend—from her *business* address?
- An offer to sell your house with one of your customer's names at the bottom of his real estate form letter?
- An important message from your CPA—full of misspellings?

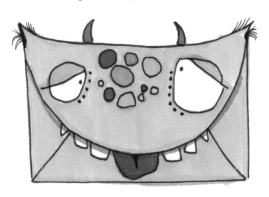

No.

And I can hear you asking me: How does email etiquette relate to customer service? Well, a lot. Emails, more than almost any other form of communication, are fraught with the potential to be misunderstood. Email recipients cannot hear tone of voice, nor see the I'm-just-kidding grin, or the thumbs-up signal. Email etiquette affects both your external customer and, especially, your internal customer—your coworkers, superiors, and underlings.

So here are some basic tips:

- Get permission before you send emails to a customer. I ordered an item from a national retailer and have been getting emails every day since. I was sure I checked the "Do Not Contact Me" box, so I don't know what happened. But I'm off their list now, forever.
- Make sure your email includes a professional greeting and a courteous closing.
- Address your contact with the appropriate level of formality and make sure you spelled the name correctly.
- Spell-check. And if this one is really important, have someone else read it before you hit send. I sent an email to someone recommending "a tear-jerker film." I typed a "t" instead of the "r" in "tear." This, uh, changed the meaning just a tad. I didn't catch it, nor did my spell-check. But she did.
- Grammar check! I received an email that a school sent out and someone returned it (using Reply All!) with the mistakes circled. Typos and grammatical mistakes are embarrassing enough, but sent from a school it is nearly unforgiveable.
- Read your email out loud to ensure the tone is appropriate. Yes, words and phrases, even punctuation, can convey tone.
- Separate your thoughts into paragraphs to make it easier to read. Stream-of-consciousness messages might be artsy and cool, but they are also impractical and inefficient.
- Keep emails brief and to the point. Save long conversations for the telephone. I don't have time for long emails, and I'm sure you don't either.
- Refrain from using the "Reply All" button. Careers have been ruined,

lives have been altered, lunch dates have been lost . . . Need I go on?

- Reply promptly. Just because someone doesn't ask for a response doesn't mean you can ignore them.
- Be sure the Subject Line accurately reflects the content of your email. Shipwrecked! is not a good subject line for a message about an error in shipping (or maybe it is . . .).
- Don't hesitate to say "Thank you," "How are you," or "Appreciate your help!"
- Be careful of using ALL CAPS. All caps are commonly understood to mean you are yelling. If you want to yell, by all means, use all caps. But if you just want to emphasize a word or phrase, bold it or italicize it or both. But don't use all caps.

CAPS LOCK
UNLEASH THE MOTHER F██KING FURY

I love this! It makes me laugh. But I do know someone who got written up for using all caps. It was considered aggressive, and it was, even though the writer didn't know it. Now you do.

- Use gender neutral language when you're not sure.
- Don't use urgent, priority, or red flags unless it really is a big deal on a short time frame.
- Consider carefully before discussing and sending confidential information. I know a health insurance broker who sent out an email to forty of his clients and friends, including me. The email contained the personal financial information of another client, including her social security number and other highly sensitive (identity theft-worthy) data. I'm certain it was sent in error but it was a 40-fold mistake that drastically reduced his credibility . . . and his client list.
- I have a five-minute delay on my email transmissions. So when I hit send too fast I can retrieve it. I've hit send more than a few times and simultaneously noticed a big mistake (or the wrong recipient!) I didn't catch on first read. That delay helps me save face.
- Your email signature should not be longer than five lines. And don't

just sign it "Sarah". I know a lot of Sarahs.

• Use common sense. I taught a class for a government entity and one of the attendees sent an email to me, with a funny but very blue video attached. Underneath was his signature, his rank, and the name of the military base. If I had forwarded that message, it would have gone global in a matter of days, even hours. I showed discretion, but he risked having an inappropriate message go out to hundreds of people with his name, rank, and location stamped on it. Good thing I liked him.

• This is my rule: Imagine reading the email you sent read aloud in a courtroom. If you're good with that, then go ahead, press send.

Do YOU have an
automatic signature
on your emails?
Do your employees?
Is it longer than
five lines in length?

Do you use
appropriate discretion
with urgent or priority
flagging of YOUR
outgoing emails?

What will YOU stop doing
as a result of
reading this chapter?

Chapter 28

Telephone Interactions

"Hello {big sigh}, may I help you?" Ever heard that when calling a business on the phone? Worse yet, you dial the number, someone picks up, but no one says anything. Instead, what you hear are muffled words or a series of clicks and then finally, someone answers with a frantic "Yes, hello?!" Bad start. Very bad start.

We've learned that nonverbal body language is important in our face-to-face interactions. In fact, 93% of the information gained during an in-person conversation is through body language. But did you know that even on the phone, nonverbal communication counts more than the words do? Your tone, inflection, pitch, rate, and volume all play a part in what the caller hears; in fact, these nonverbal elements account for a whopping 80% of it.

My tips:

Answer the phone professionally. I have occasionally apologized for getting a wrong number when dialing a business whose phone is answered with just a "hello." I hang up, check the number, and dial again, only to find I did get the right number but because it was not answered with "ACME tree trimming; may I help you?" I thought I had gotten Joe Schmo out of bed. Saying the name of your business first is a good rule of thumb. Whatever comes next can vary. Confession here: I routinely answer my phone by saying "This is Jean." I'm changing it today to "Happy People Win. This is Jean." (I always learn something when I write new material.) Hey, maybe I should have Pharrell's "Happy" playing in the background, or use it for my on-hold music. What do you think?

I won't divulge the company's name, but one of the businesses I work with answers its phones with "It's a great day at ACME Assisted Living!" It always makes me laugh, because sometimes their tone of voice suggests they are so NOT having a great day—at all. Don't be hokey. And don't make your greeting a long one. "Thank you for calling ACME Toy Store where today we're running a special on train sets just come in between 10 am and 5 pm and ask for Gerry the new Barbie dolls are going fast may I help you?" No thanks. Remind me not to call again. Plus, I feel for the employees who have to rattle it off every time.

The Dreaded Phone Tree

Copyright © by Randy Glasbergen.
www.glasbergen.com

**"Please listen carefully as some of our menu options
have changed. For customer service, go fly a kite.
For technical support, whistle in the wind until
the cows come home. For repair service, wait
for you-know-what to freeze over...."**

Data shows it's far more likely you'll get a phone tree than a live person at the typical customer service department. No surprise here. I'm used to it, but I still don't like it and I'm guessing neither do you.

Brad Tuttle at *Time Magazine* said it wonderfully: *"The ninth circle of customer service hell usually begins with a phone call looped through a maddeningly automated system known as IVR (Interactive Voice Response)—you know, the one in which you 'Press 1 to continue in English' and 'Listen closely to our list of options, as they may have changed.' Turns out, not all Internet retailers use such systems. Instead, many top retailers utilize what's known as 'live human beings' to answer the phone."*

"Perhaps most surprising of all," he adds, *"the companies that employ living breathing customer service reps to answer phones also tend to have shorter wait times for callers."*

Here's an excerpt from *CNN Money.*

"In order to expedite your call, please choose from the following menu. Press 1 to place an order. Press 2 for questions about existing orders. Press 3 for questions about your credit card. Press 4 for billing information."

Aaaaaand where's the option for "none of the above"?

Way too many companies don't offer one, which means you make the wrong choice and land in purgatory, unable to get back to the main menu. Sometimes the only thing to do is to hang up and try again. Frustrating is an understatement.

But automatic answering systems aren't necessarily a bad thing, said Micah Solomon, author of High-Tech, High-Touch Customer Service. The problem occurs when you can't escape the automation and just speak to a human.

"Setting it up so that it becomes a voice jail not only hurts your customers, but it hurts your brand,"

It's a wonder those of us who end up yelling back at the automated voices ("No, I do NOT wish to pay my bill; I wish to CANCEL my effing membership!") aren't all in a special rubber room for telephone tree abusers. Honestly.

A very successful restaurant has an automated telephone tree with four options, the final one being this one: "If you wish to speak with a living breathing person, press 4." Believe it or not, some people like pressing buttons to make reservations, and especially to cancel them. So option four is not used as  often as you might think. And it certainly strengthens their already solid customer base.

Beyond that?

- Answer promptly. There is one business I am forced to call; they are the only option I have. I count the rings, usually over 20, before someone picks up. If a competitor ever hits town, they'll be toast. Three rings is the acceptable standard.

- Before you answer: Stop other conversations, stop typing, and spit out your gum.

- Start with a smile in your voice. Physically smiling really helps with this. People can hear you smile. It's a proven fact. Smiling raises the soft palate at the back of your mouth and makes your sound waves more fluid, so smiling makes you sound more open and friendly. According to a piece that aired on the Discovery Channel, human beings can differentiate vocal intonation not only between a smile and a non-smile but among different *types* of smiles. Who knew?

- It doesn't take long for a customer to pick up on your attitude. Whether you're bored brainless, jumpy as a nervous cricket, or just married and loving every minute of it—they can hear it within seconds.

- Direct people to the right resources. Have the numbers readily available. Before you transfer them, give them the number to which you are sending them in case they are disconnected.

- Put the caller on hold smoothly. Not "City Water Department please hold"—click. Wait for me to answer.

- Sound alive, not scripted. I've actually waited for the beep following a welcome message from a live person because it sounded so robotic.

- Be patient. How do you signify impatience on the phone? Sighing; interrupting; the quick, repetitive "yeh, yeh, yeh."

- Tune into your speaker's tone. Case in point: I called to order an item and was pleased to get someone in the U.S., someone with one of those gracious, thick Southern accents, no less. I told him how nice it was and he said, "Ma'am, I'm actually in India. We just learned

Southern accents to make people happy." I was so surprised, I couldn't respond so he quickly added, "Just joshing with you." I loved it. Someone in a pissy mood might not. I think he knew I would laugh. And that's called tuning in to your speaker's tone. If someone sounds cranky, don't try to be funny.

• If your time is short, say so. Sometimes that doesn't work but it's good to try it first, before you hang up on them. I was talking to a government agency once whose brand new rep was under trained and over her head. I was in a huge hurry and told her I'd find the information online instead. I had to tell her twice. Then I had to hang up.

Lastly, if you have to leave a message on a machine, please . . .

• Enunciate clearly
• Moderate your voice volume
• State your name and number at the beginning of the message and repeat both at the end of it
• Don't assume they know how to spell your name
• Don't assume they are in the same area code

Does YOUR company
have a standard
telephone greeting?
Is it mandated or agreed
upon by staff?

If your company
has a phone tree,
is there an option
for a customer to speak
to a live person?
If no, why not?

Chapter 29

The Passive Aggressive Trap
Or . . . Don't be a D**k

"Behind the smile, a hidden knife!"
~ Chinese proverb

My sister Suzie called me a few weeks ago. Mad. Really mad. She had had an appointment with her dog groomer and didn't get her usual guy. So she introduced herself and her dog, Otto, to the new guy. "Sorry, we can't take him," he said, after looking Otto over and discovering some knots in his belly hair. "What?" she asked, incredulous that a dog groomer couldn't take a regular customer for, uh, let's see, what is his business? Oh yeah . . . dog grooming! He wouldn't cut them out (he claimed he had no scissors) and he wouldn't let Suzie do it, either. Finally, the new guy picks up little Otto and says in a high, sweet voice, "Well, Otto, I will do this, but I hope you don't hate me for making you hurt so much. It will be very painful being groomed with these terrible knots."

Be Alert For Passive Aggressive People

Suzie was furious. But I was thrilled to get such a fabulous example of classic passive-aggressive behavior for my workshops.

Maybe the new guy was in a bad mood; maybe he was overwhelmed with appointments. Perhaps he didn't like to deal with hair knots. Or maybe he was angry with Suzie for allowing the knots to happen in the first place (hello, that's why she was there!). Who knows? We'll never know how he really felt or why, because he didn't tell the truth. Instead, he took whatever he was feeling (and not saying) out on Suzie and Otto. In telling the story to me, Suzie's parting suggestion was to title this book, "Don't be a D**khead!". So I'm naming a chapter in homage to her and as a caution to you: Be aware of your passive-aggressive behavior (feeling one thing and doing another) and please, don't be a d**khead.

Psychology Today writes: *"The customer service industry is especially ripe for situational passive-aggressive behaviors in that service professionals are expected to demonstrate hospitable behaviors at all times. When faced with demanding patrons and customers, these workers may maintain their public smile while privately seething and plotting revenge."*

What this piece refers to is a thing called "the angry smile," a term coined by Signe Whitson. It happens when employees with poor coping skills can't handle a bad situation or even their own bad mood. I met such a woman . . .

It was a hard winter day and I had just checked into a very nice hotel. On the way to my room, bags in tow, a guest pointed out that one of my bags was open and was trailing the items that had fallen out of it. Arrgghh! A few miles back, I had unzipped it at a rest stop and in my haste to get out of the storm, I just grabbed it and hauled it inside. So I thanked my fellow guest, let myself into my room, took a quick inventory, and realized I was missing my red makeup bag. Whereupon I ran downstairs, inspected my car, pawed in the snow, and retraced my steps. Nothing.

"Please tell me someone brought in a red makeup bag from the parking lot in the last ten minutes," I begged the reception clerk who had just checked me in. She gave me the Angry Smile and asked me what it looked like and what was inside. I was tempted to say "condoms and heroin" but she wasn't in a mood for my humor. "Come on," I implored. "How many red makeup bags were turned in from the parking lot in the last ten minutes?" She ignored me (the angry smile frozen on her face) and retreated into a backroom. A full five minutes later, she returned and handed me my bag (the red one, with makeup in it). So I asked again, "Okay, all joking aside, how many red makeup bags were turned in since I got here?" "Three," she announced, like her hand was on a Bible. In retrospect, I should have said, "Well, then. It's a true miracle you were able to choose, out of three red makeup bags, the one that is mine." But at that point, I was stupefied by the fact that she could lie so easily, angry smile or not.

Passive aggressive (PA) is a communication style, a personality type, and some say a disorder—one that is characterized by indirect resistance and veiled hostility. Or it can manifest in innuendo, not-too-subtle digs, and "playful" teasing. Urban dictionary adds, *"A defense mechanism that allows people who aren't comfortable being openly aggressive get what they want under the guise of trying to please others. They want their way, but they also want everyone to like them."*

In the world of customer service, employees with PA can be outrageously rude, but they hide it under a pile of sugary sweet condescension. Dr. Martin Seidenfeld calls it **covert abuse** and says, *"Covert abuse is hard to deal with. When someone hits you or yells at you, you know you're being abused. But covert abuse is subtle and veiled or disguised by actions that appear to be normal; at times, even kind and caring. The PA is a master of covert abuse."*

If you are not the passive-aggressive person, here are some valuable tips to help you cope with those who are.

- *Don't overreact or personalize the PA's behavior.* I once told an assertive training class a story about one of my college professor's passive-aggressive husband. He would conveniently "forget" to give her messages from the women friends he didn't like. After sharing the story, a man in my class announced he was guilty. Why? He forgets to give his wife messages. On purpose? No, he just forgets. That's called forgetful, not passive-aggressive. Look for a pattern.

- *Don't try to change them.* You are not a psychotherapist.

- *Ask for things in writing.*

- *Don't play the game.* Using the same sweetly-rendered sarcasm back at them is not the answer.

- *Be assertive.* Focus on your feelings. Tell the person his statement or behavior feels uncomfortable or hurts your feelings. Ask him not to repeat the behavior or comment. Or ask: "That sounded like a dig. Did you mean it that way?"

And please . . . don't be a d**k.

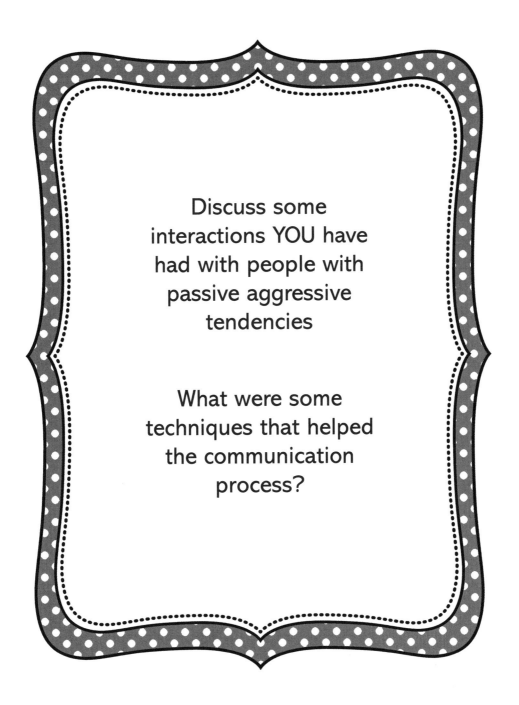

Discuss some
interactions YOU have
had with people with
passive aggressive
tendencies

What were some
techniques that helped
the communication
process?

Chapter 30

Make 'Em Laugh:

The Role of Humor in Customer Service

"As you know, it's a no-smoking, no-whining, no-complaining flight," Marty Cobb, a flight attendant on Southwest Airlines told passengers. "It's a 'please' and 'thank you' and 'you are such a good looking flight attendant' flight." Marty's safety announcement went viral, as did David Holmes's rapping safety talk, another Southwest flight attendant. When *Huffington Post* writes an article on "The Coolest Southwest Airlines Flight Attendants," you *know* you're doing something right.

I love laughing. When stuff happens, I have a choice: to laugh or to cry. I prefer the former. I use a lot of humor in my talks; not telling jokes per se, but sharing funny stories or situations. And guess what? People love to laugh. So much so that I often get requests to speak without a topic. "Just be funny," they say. (FYI, I never do it, ever. I am not a comedian.)

Forbes wrote: *"Tasteful humor is a key to success at work, but there's a good chance your co-workers aren't cracking jokes or packaging information with wit on a regular basis—and your office could probably stand to have a little more fun."*

Customer Experience Insight shares a study where " . . . *salespeople sent a non-offensive Dilbert cartoon to prospects early in the sales process and ahead of a lengthy, somewhat complex contract. Another group of salespeople sent the contract without the cartoon. The group that sent the cartoon generated higher levels of trust with customers and saw a 15% better return, plus increased customer satisfaction.*"

Humor can:

- improve sales
- improve customer loyalty
- help you stand out

Why aren't people laughing more in your workplace? Some people worry it might offend someone; others don't want to be the first person who tries it and are afraid they might not be funny. There is also a concern that your customers won't find the humor in what *you* think is funny. It could happen. There's no one-size-fits-all kind of humor, so make sure you get feedback before you start doling out fart cushions to prospective clients.

I don't think you can mandate fun, and scripting it can be uncomfortable. However, I do believe there are opportunities in every business to incorporate fun into the customer service experience. If you don't believe me, watch a few episodes of *Six Feet Under*. Besides being brilliantly written, this TV show demonstrates that even those who run a mortuary, those who deal with death and grief all day, every day, can find something to laugh about. (Among themselves of course. Not with the grieving relatives . . . or the corpses. That would be just . . . wrong.)

Humor can help build relationships, and isn't that what you want with your customers?

How do YOU respond
to humor in professional
interactions?
In the sales process?

Does YOUR company
support the element
of humor in customer
interactions?

How do YOU respond
when you might have gone
too far?

Chapter 31

Stress, Burnout, & Clients from Hell

If you've never had a customer from hell, call me. There might be a Guinness World Record in the making. We've all had them, right? Those clients, patients, or customers who make us a little crazy, no matter what we do.

> **Client**: The picture seems really yellow and orange.
>
> **Graphic Artist**: Well it's a sunset.
>
> **Client**: Right. But could you make the center thing less yellow/orange?
>
> **Graphic Artist**: You mean the sun?
>
> **Client**: Yeah. Let me think about a different color other than yellow and orange. Maybe green?

> ~ clientsfromhell.net

© Randy Glasbergen
glasbergen.com

GLASBERGEN

"I guess things have been kind of stressful at the office.
Tomorrow is Bring Your Therapist To Work Day."

Adding insult to injury (in hospitals that figurative phrase becomes *literally* true), some jobs are inherently stressful; if you're an ER nurse or an airline pilot, stress comes with the territory. So what to do about it?

Some things to remember:

- Troublesome people are few and far between.
- You are a professional
- Maintain perspective
- Don't take it personally
- Remain calm
- Take a time out
- Develop stress reduction strategies

Preempt the day, or customer, from hell by taking care of yourself. You can only serve as good as you feel.

I don't believe there's such a thing as perfect work/life balance. It's about progress, not perfection, so here's how to get a lot better at it:

- Build downtime into your schedule
- Take your vacations

- Start small, build from there. Like leaving the office early one night per week
- Let go of perfectionism (but strive for excellence)
- Unplug and step away from email
- Find something to relax you: running, meditation, reading, cooking, yoga
- Say "no"
- Limit people and activities that are time-wasters

When you take steps to intentionally reduce on-the-job stress; when you seek and practice ways to mitigate the damaging effects of difficult customers, you are less likely to burn out—and *far* less likely to blaze out!

All of which can do nothing but enhance the quality of your customer service. Think of the hammock as job security; the yoga class as a way to increase company profits; the newest Anne Lamott novel as a remedy for departmental overload. And that French cooking class? *Quel* client difficile? (translation: *What* difficult customer?

What are some
stress reduction strategies
that YOU use?
Are there some that
you as a group
can do together?

Do you use YOUR
PTO (paid time off)?
Are employees
at your business
encouraged to do so?

Getting to Great . . .

& Staying There

In *Need Change?* pages, I've packed a career's worth of study, stats, and stories on the often-neglected but vitally important topic of customer service. It's been quite the journey for me. I started with the belief that I did not "do" customer service, and ended with more than 30 chapters on the subject.

I work with businesses of all types and sizes every day, and every day I add another story, another idea to the heap. I have always been keenly aware of how we treat each other as human beings, and customer service is just an extension of that. My hope is that you, too, will become hyper-sensitive about customer service so that more of us will receive what we deserve at the places where we spend our hard-earned dollars.

It's fun, even exciting, to implement the policies and ideas that take your customer service from good to great. The difficulty is in maintaining it. So I encourage you to pick a chapter and make them a regular part of your staff or marketing meetings, workshops, and refresher courses.

There should also be:

- Written polices around customer service
- Staff trainings
- Continual feedback from customers
- Recognition for excellent service
- Customer service feedback as part of employees' annual review

It's like wellness. You don't just arrive at total wellness at, say, 36 years of age and call it a day. It's a continual process. With regular maintenance. More study. And ongoing discussion.

I began with a quote from Aristotle. Let me end with a quote from speaker Dottie Walters: *"Success is not a doorway, it's a stairway."*

I hope you will use *Need Change?* as another flight of stairs as you rise to the top of your industry. Happy climbing.

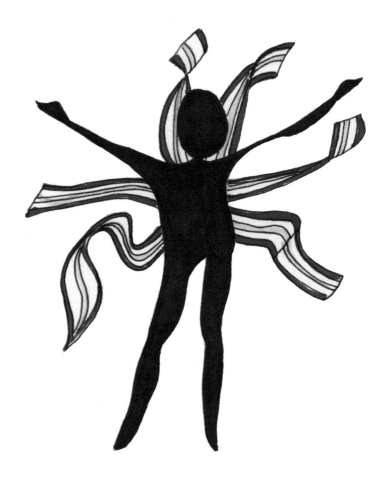

About the Author

Born in L.A. and raised in Africa and Asia, Jean Steel's unique life perspective has been healing sick companies, and inspiring individuals for over 20 years. Moving frequently and changing schools often, she developed strength, resilience, flexibility and a keen appreciation for life.

Jean graduated from the University of California at Santa Barbara with a degree in Sociology, and then worked for ten years as a health educator in a drug and alcohol center. In Sacramento, California, she designed a preventative medicine program for Kaiser Permanente. Jean earned her Master's Degree from Sacramento State in Mind & Body Health and Wellness, a program she designed herself. With a long and prestigious list of clients that includes hospitals, universities, cities, and internationally known corporations, Jean's work has had a major impact on the productivity and quality of work delivered, and has enriched the working lives of countless corporate staff. Her talks have also inspired small businesses and individuals working in difficult, stressful environments. Self-responsibility, the power of choice, and the art of mindfulness are a few of the themes guiding her powerful, interactive talks and seminars. Humor is a hallmark, and no one delivers a story with more down-home hilarity than Jean Steel. She is the founder/Queen/President/CEO of Happy People Win, home of Happy Nurses Win and Happy Employees Win.

About the Illustrator

Illustrator Suz Steel Roehl, is Jean's middle sister. A flight nurse by trade for CALSTAR—California Shock Trauma Air Rescue—she also competes in 3-day cross country events (riding one of her three horses), and follows her passions for gardening, traveling, hiking, and making a mean margarita. She lives with her husband Rick and her two sons Alec and Tony on the Central Coast of California.